CONTENTS

**Institute of Terrestrial Ecology**

M
fo

the
UNIVERSITY
of
GREENWICH

Natural Environment Research Council

**Institute of
Terrestrial
Ecology**

Managing set-aside land for wildlife

ITE research publication no. 7

L G Firbank, H R Arnold, B C Eversham,
J O Mountford, G L Radford, M G Telfer,
J R Treweek, N R C Webb and T C E Wells

LONDON: HMSO   Natural Environment Research Council

The Institute of Terrestrial Ecology (ITE) is a component research organisation within the Natural Environment Research Council. The Institute is part of the Terrestrial and Freshwater Sciences Directorate, and was established in 1973 by the merger of the research stations of the Nature Conservancy with the Institute of Tree Biology. It has been at the forefront of ecological research ever since. The six research stations of the Institute provide a ready access to sites and to environmental and ecological problems in any part of Britain. In addition to the broad environmental knowledge and experience expected of the modern ecologist, each station has a range of special expertise and facilities. Thus, the Institute is able to provide unparallelled opportunities for long-term, multidisciplinary studies of complex environmental and ecological problems.

ITE undertakes specialist ecological research on subjects ranging from micro-organisms to trees and mammals, from coastal habitats to uplands, from derelict land to air pollution. Understanding the ecology of different species of natural and man-made communities plays an increasingly important role in areas such as monitoring ecological aspects of agriculture, improving productivity in forestry, controlling pests, managing and conserving wildlife, assessing the causes and effects of pollution, and rehabilitating disturbed sites.

The Institute's research is financed by the UK Government through the science budget, and by private and public sector customers who commission or sponsor specific research programmes. ITE's expertise is also widely used by international organisations in overseas collaborative projects.

The results of ITE research are available to those responsible for the protection, management and wise use of our natural resources, being published in a wide range of scientific journals, and in an ITE series of publications. The Annual Report contains more general information.

L G Firbank, H R Arnold, B C Eversham, J O Mountford, J R Treweek and T C E Wells
ITE, Monks Wood, Abbots Ripton, Huntingdon, Cambridgeshire PE17 2LS
Tel: 048 73 381

G L Radford
ITE, Bangor Research Unit, University College of North Wales, Deiniol Road, Bangor, Gwynedd LL57 2UP
Tel: 0248 370045

M G Telfer
ITE, Monks Wood; present address: School of Environmental Sciences, University of East Anglia, Norwich, Norfolk NR4 7TJ
Tel: 0603 56161

N R C Webb
ITE, Furzebrook Research Station, Wareham, Dorset BH20 5AS
Tel: 0929 551518

PREFACE

The Common Agricultural Policy was reformed in 1992, and one of the major effects was to increase dramatically the extent of arable land being set aside. A second feature was the provision for an agri-environment scheme supporting long-term habitat creation and management on farmland taken out of production. In the summer of 1992, the Institute of Terrestrial Ecology was contracted by the Ministry of Agriculture, Fisheries and Food to investigate the possibilities of using set-aside arable land for the benefit of wildlife. The precise objectives of the review were:

- to produce a list of habitat types of value for wildlife which could benefit from long-term set-aside;

- to produce a list of species currently at reduced levels which could benefit from long term set-aside – the list to be cross-referenced by habitat requirements;

- for each habitat selected under the first objective, to specify criteria for site selection, implications of different management options and opportunities for assessment; and also to indicate possible off-site impacts of the management options;

- for those species noted under the second objective which require particular conditions beyond those covered by the third objective, to specify criteria for site selection, implications of different management options and opportunities for assessments; and also to indicate the possible off-site impacts of the management options.

The second objective turned out to be impracticable, because of the large numbers of species involved. Therefore, emphasis switched to declines within groups of species in Great Britain, with special reference to England. In addition, rotational set-aside was included because of its potential value for species and habitat conservation. The report (Firbank *et al.* 1992[*]) was delivered at the end of 1992, and was used in conjunction with other sources to develop the range of set-aside and agri-environmental programmes for 1993 and 1994.

One of the priorities identified was to publicise the details of the management proposals for the benefit of farmers and their advisors. This book is an attempt to address this need. The early part of the report, relating to choice of schemes, has been completely rewritten for a more general audience, but our recommendations for habitat management have been revised only slightly.

We must stress that the research base for environmental set-aside is slight. Much of what we have written is based on experience from other situations, and may not turn out to encompass the most effective ways of managing set-aside. A recommendation of the report was for a system of monitoring and review in order to improve the advice available; this book represents only a first step towards providing a comprehensive guide for managing set-aside land for wildlife.

*Firbank, L.G., Arnold, H.R., Eversham, B.C., Mountford, J.O., Radford, G.L., Telfer, M.G., Treweek, J.R., Webb, N.R.C. & Wells, T.C.E. 1992. *The potential uses of set-aside land to benefit wildlife.* (NERC contract report to the Ministry of Agriculture, Fisheries and Food.) Abbots Ripton, Huntingdon: Institute of Terrestrial Ecology.

ACKNOWLEDGEMENTS

We thank Sarah Hendry, Judy Allfrey, Patrice Mongelard and
Dr J E King from the Ministry of Agriculture, Fisheries and Food who
managed the project which led to this book. They have been
consistently helpful and constructive throughout the development of
the work. We thank Laurie Boorman, Jane Croft, Brian Davis, John
Good, Shelley Hinsley, Paul Harding, Mark Hill, Dorian Moss, Chris
Preston and Rob Rose, all staff of ITE, for their own contributions and
comments.

We are also grateful to the following people for having discussed with
us our report to MAFF:

> Nigel Boatman, Game Conservancy
> Len Campbell, Royal Society for the Protection of Birds
> Andy Evans, Royal Society for the Protection of Birds
> Karen Goodwin, English Nature
> Rowena Langston, British Trust for Ornithology
> Stephen Rumsey, farm owner, Icklesham
> Alistair Rutherford, Countryside Commission
> Helen Smith, University of Oxford
> Juliet Vickery, University of East Anglia
> Philip Wayre, Otter Trust.

We do not claim to represent their views, and any mistakes in this
book remain the sole responsibility of the authors.

SET-ASIDE AND WILDLIFE

1 INTRODUCTION

The set-aside programme

A cornerstone of the Common Agricultural Policy (CAP) of the European Community (EC) is to provide price support for farmers. This policy proved such an effective incentive that, by 1986, surplus stocks had increased to the point where the cost of their storage and disposal was so high that it was suggested that it would be cheaper to pay the farmers not to grow the surplus in the first place (Floyd 1992). A voluntary set-aside programme for arable farming lasting for five years was approved in February 1988, and introduced in time for the 1989 harvest. The economic purpose of set-aside was to remove land from agricultural production, while keeping it in sound condition for agriculture in the future. However, by 1992, it was clear that the 'take-up' by farmers was small (less than 2 million ha in the EC) and that the potential savings had been outweighed by the cost of managing the scheme (Floyd 1992).

In 1992, the Common Agricultural Policy was reformed in an attempt to tackle its growing costs, and, as part of this reform, the role of set-aside was dramatically enlarged. It now covers an area of approximately 600 000 ha in the UK, greater than all nature reserves put together (Wilson & Fuller 1992), and represents a great change in the use of land in the lowlands. Larger arable farmers are now required to set-aside 15% of their arable land to qualify for support, which takes the form of payments on the basis of area rather than on production (Ministry of Agriculture, Fisheries and Food (MAFF) 1992, 1993a). Land in the 1988 scheme can stay in that scheme, or be transferred to the new scheme. To prevent farmers putting only their worst land into set-aside, the new scheme requires a six-year rotation of set-aside around the arable area of the farm. Land set-aside in 1992 is permitted to enter as non-rotational set-aside in 1993. Other programmes will also be introduced in 1994 as part of the EC's agri-environment package, notably a Countryside Access Scheme and a longer-term (at least 20 years) Habitat Scheme.

A number of rules for set-aside in 1993 have not been finalised by the EC at the time of writing. However, the explanatory guides available to farmers (MAFF 1993a,b) make clear the following conditions.

For all set-aside

- The minimum plot size is 0.3 ha, unless bounded by permanent features, and the minimum width is 20 m.
- There can be no agricultural production except for certain non-food crops and unharvestable mixtures (eg for game cover). Grazing by farm animals is allowed only to a very limited extent. The farmer will be committed to maintain good cropping conditions.
- Environmental and archaeological features on or adjacent to set-aside land must not be damaged or destroyed.
- While public access may be permitted on set-aside land, there may be no profit for the farmer.
- Under certain circumstances, farmers can obtain derogations from set-aside rules for conservation and other purposes.

For rotational set-aside

- 15% of arable land must be set-aside for all but the smallest farms, and so 90% of the arable land of the farm will have been entered by the end of the six-year rotation. The rules apply from 15 January to 31 August, with restrictions on the use of the land up to 14 January of the following year.
- A green cover must be established, by sowing or natural regeneration, unless the previous crop was harvested after the beginning of October. Sown covers must not be suitable for cropping or seed production, and legumes should not normally

exceed 5% of the seed mixture. The cover must be destroyed by 31 August, or cut between 15 July and 15 August. Derogations can be sought to protect wildlife.

- Insecticides and fungicides can only be applied under specific exemptions. Non-residual herbicides can be used, but non-selective herbicides must not be used to destroy the cover before 15 April. Fertilizers cannot be applied, except for moderate levels of slurry and manure from the same farm. Liming is permitted.

For non-rotational set-aside

- Entry into non-rotational set-aside programmes will require 18% of the arable area to be set-aside to account for farmers setting aside their least productive land; this value may be revised after two years. The commitment will last for at least five years (although there is limited scope for opting out, including at the end of 1993–94 because of continued uncertainty over some of the rules), and the rules for non-rotational set-aside will apply for the whole of this time.

- Fertilizers, manure and slurry can be used only for non-food options, or with a derogation. Non-residual herbicides can be used, providing the green cover is not destroyed (except to replace with another green cover). Other herbicides, insecticides and fungicides can be used only with a derogation.

- Non-rotational set-aside must be managed specifically as field margin, grassland, natural regeneration, wild bird cover, non-food crop, or an option proposed by the farmer.

- Suitable land may be entered into the proposed Countryside Access Scheme expected in 1994.

For the Countryside Access Scheme, there will be additional payments. The following rules are expected to apply.

- Free public access is provided, but no new permanent rights of way are created. Existing rights of way are not covered.

- The land must be entered into the non-rotational set-aside scheme, and set-aside rules apply.

- Payments will be for 10 m wide access strips as well as larger areas of land.

From 1994, there is expected to be a separate 20-year Habitat Scheme, and the following rules are anticipated.

- The scheme will apply to all agricultural land, not just arable land. The scheme is intrinsically separate from the set-aside programme, and so the arable set-aside rules need not apply.
- If changes to EC legislation permit Habitat Scheme land to be counted as part of the non-rotational set-aside requirement, then the appropriate set-aside rules will have to be observed.
- Fertilizers and pesticides cannot be used without derogations. Vernacular, environmental and archaeological features must be preserved. Limited grazing may be allowed at non-commercial levels.
- The following options will be available: intertidal habitats, notably salt marsh; water fringe habitats (in designated areas only); and management of particularly valuable habitats established under the five-year set-aside scheme. Further options for the restoration of lowland heath and lowland damp grassland are also proposed if such land is allowed to count as set-aside.

Some major questions remain unresolved by the EC at the time of writing. In particular, it has yet to decide the conditions under which farmers can enter land into both rotational and non-rotational schemes, and current rules do not allow land under the Farm Woodland Premium Scheme and the proposed Habitat Scheme to count as set-aside land (although the UK Government is pressing for a change). These issues may affect the take-up of the different schemes considerably.

Set-aside and the environment

While the prime objective of set-aside is to reduce food production (Floyd 1992), it affects landscape and wildlife greatly. Under the 1988 scheme, untidy, weedy fields contrasted sharply with the tidy landscapes resulting from modern intensive farming. However, on some set-aside land, wildlife began to flourish. Rare weed species were seen in substantial numbers. Birds used the set-aside land, especially weedy winter stubbles. Under the experimental Countryside Premium Scheme in East Anglia, set-aside was turned into new habitats, including alternative feeding areas for Brent geese (*Branta bernicla bernicla*), and public access areas were established, creating meadow walks around villages previously hemmed in by intensive arable land (Ewins & Roberts 1992). Concern by farmers that set-aside would result in dramatic weed, pest and disease problems turned out to be largely unjustified (Clarke 1992), as did concerns by environmentalists that farmers would manage their remaining land more intensively (Ansell & Tranter 1992).

The experience of the Countryside Premium Scheme has encouraged MAFF to try to persuade farmers to manage set-aside land to improve the environmental quality of the countryside. Environmental quality has proved difficult to define, which is not surprising considering the range of aspects in the environment and the subjective nature of evaluating them. For example, some people perceive a closely mown grass sward as being of higher quality than a weedy stubble, because it looks tidier and better managed. However, other people would prefer the stubble because of its greater abundance of birds, insects and flowers.

Experience within the United States and in Europe shows that environmental concerns can be met within set-aside programmes (Ervin 1992; Ewins & Roberts 1992). Potential objectives include:

- to conserve wildlife

- to promote biological control of pests on nearby arable land

- to increase stocks of game and fish

- to reduce groundwater pollution

- to manage runoff of nutrients and agrochemicals into adjacent water and land

- to provide public access and amenity

- to improve rural landscapes

- to reduce carbon dioxide emissions

- to replace fossil by biomass fuels.

This book concentrates on the first objective; other environmental options are not considered, except where the promotion of species and habitats coincides or conflicts with other environmental objectives. We deal largely with set-aside in the lowlands, to reflect the distribution of most arable land, but the Habitat Scheme and set-aside may also have significant benefits to wildlife and the rural landscape in the uplands and elsewhere by supporting differential, reduced and zero grazing regimes.

Managing set-aside land for wildlife involves the setting of objectives, in exactly the same way as managing for agricultural production. If benefits for wildlife are to be regarded as the 'product', then the decision must be made as to which wildlife. This decision depends upon national and regional priorities for conservation, and upon the local opportunities within the farm itself. Given the choice between a grass monoculture and a weedy stubble, we would recommend the weedy stubble, unless the stubble was of particularly low quality (ie full of species of little value in themselves or to other species, such as couch-grass (*Elymus repens*)), or the grass was of particularly high quality (eg if it was being managed as pasture for geese).

Having decided upon the general objectives, then details of day-to-day management have to be considered. There is no fundamental difference between raising sheep and raising stone curlews (*Burhinus oedicnemus*), or between growing continuous cereals and growing lowland heath. It should be remembered that many of the habitats discussed in this book have in the past depended upon agriculture – they do not present an entirely novel set of management problems for farmers, although there are new conditions arising from the set-aside rules, the more mechanised farming system in which set-aside is unlikely to take a high priority, and the recent intensive management on much set-aside land.

References

Ansell, D.J. & Tranter, R.B. 1992. *Set-aside: in theory and in practice.* Reading: Centre for Agricultural Strategy, University of Reading.

Clarke, J., ed. 1992. *Set-aside.* Farnham: British Crop Protection Council.

Ervin, D. 1992. Some lessons about the political-economic effects of set-aside: the United States' experience. In: *Set-aside*, edited by J. Clarke, 3–12. Farnham: British Crop Protection Council.

Ewins, A.E. & Roberts, R.J. 1992. The countryside premium scheme for set-aside land. In: *Set-aside*, edited by J. Clarke, 229–234. Farnham: British Crop Protection Council.

Floyd, W.D. 1992. Political aspects of set aside as a policy instrument in the European Community. In: *Set-aside*, edited by J. Clarke, 13–20. Farnham: British Crop Protection Council.

Ministry of Agriculture, Fisheries and Food. 1992. *Area arable payments: explanatory booklet.* London: MAFF.

Ministry of Agriculture, Fisheries and Food. 1993a. *Arable area payments 1993/94. Explanatory guide: Part I.* London: MAFF.

Ministry of Agriculture, Fisheries and Food. 1993b. *Arable area payments 1993/94. Explanatory guide: Part II.* London: MAFF.

Wilson, J. & Fuller, R. 1992. Set-aside: potential and management for conservation. *Ecos,* **13**, 24–29.

2 PRIORITIES FOR CONSERVATION ON SET-ASIDE FARMLAND

The wildlife of farmland has always been in flux, as farming techniques and intensity have changed. Some wild species of farmland, such as the grass weed, barren brome (*Bromus sterilis*), have recently increased in abundance. However, many more species have become rarer as habitats have been lost and degraded as a result of the increasing intensification and specialisation of agriculture since the Second World War. Some of these are unlikely to benefit from set-aside, either because the set-aside management is inappropriate, or the location is unsuitable or inaccessible. However, some species of national and international conservation value will be found on set-aside land, notably rare weeds and birds, and these should take a high priority in the management of set-aside on the farm.

There are several sources of information to help decide priorities for conservation, reviewed by the Nature Conservancy Council (1989). The *Red Data Books* classify species thought to be under threat of extinction into the categories 'endangered', 'vulnerable', 'rare' (implying a potential risk of extinction), 'out of danger' and 'endemic' (not thought to occur beyond Britain, and hence of international conservation value). Volumes are available so far for vascular plants (Perring & Farrell 1977, 1983), insects (Shirt 1987), other invertebrates (Bratton 1991) and birds (Batten *et al.* 1990); a substantial number of these species could benefit from restoring their habitats under set-aside. Some of these species and habitats are referred to under a range of national and international legislation, such as the Wildlife and Countryside Act 1981, Directives of the European Community, and others. For example, habitats of conservation importance listed by the EC 'Habitats Directive' (Commission of the European Communities 1992) include dry heathland, sandy grassland, calcareous grassland, lowland hay meadows and salt marsh – all of which can be restored on set-aside land.

Set-aside may prove to be suited best for increasing populations of species which are fairly widespread and can invade areas of newly restored habitats. It is, therefore, worth considering which habitats and which species have declined the most in abundance in recent times, and then to assess the prospects for helping them within set-aside programmes.

Estimates of habitat loss

Evidence for habitat loss can come from either changes in land cover or changes in species distribution. Land cover estimates can to some extent be derived from published sources, but rarely refer to changes in the overall landscape. For example, Fuller (1987) used a combination of published statistics to assess the decline of species-rich grassland, showing that, by 1984, unimproved pastures occupied only 3% of their extent in 1938. Attempts to infer habitat loss through the use of old maps and photographs are very labour-intensive, and have been restricted to particular situations, such as the loss of Dorset heath (Moore 1962; Webb & Haskins 1980; Webb 1990). When taken together, such reviews show that agriculture has been the most important factor by far in causing these changes in British vegetation since the Middle Ages (Ratcliffe 1984).

The national surveys of the Institute of Terrestrial Ecology (ITE) (Bunce, Barr & Fuller 1992; Bunce et al. 1992) were designed to provide a national picture of land cover and vegetation change. They began in 1978, long after the intensification of British agriculture, but even since then they have revealed a substantial decline in the lengths of hedgerows (Barr et al. 1991).

Estimates of decline

Even if statistics of habitat change were available, they would not necessarily show changes in habitat quality. Intensive use and neglect have both reduced the value of many habitats which remain (Rackham 1986). Therefore, statistics of species decline are arguably more useful than those of habitat decline, because they take into account both land cover and habitat quality.

Such statistics can be calculated from data held by the ITE Biological Records Centre (BRC) and the British Trust for Ornithology. The BRC was established to map the distribution of plant and animal species in Britain, with data going as far back as the early 19th century. It has grown to encompass a wide range of species-related data, including aspects of the ecology and habitat preferences of species (Harding & Sheail 1992).

There are too many species to consider each separately for setting priorities for set-aside land. However, the species can be classified according their habitat needs; if a large proportion of species belonging to a particular habitat has declined, then it is reasonable to assume that the habitat in question has itself declined, in quality or in quantity. We undertook this analysis as part of our report to MAFF (Firbank *et al.* 1992), choosing the following groups:

mammals
butterflies
larger moths
dragonflies and damselflies
grasshoppers
bumblebees
molluscs
scarce plants.

We classified the species within these groups into the following habitats which could be restored on set-aside land:

dry heathland
sandy grassland
calcareous grassland
damp grassland
salt marsh
fen and water fringe vegetation
hedgerows and small woods
woodland edge, woodland clearings and scrub
fallow fields and waste ground (eg roadside verges)
arable land.

We then looked at changes since the last century in each group of species in each habitat. We found that the ranges of rare plants have declined particularly in calcareous grassland, sandy grassland, fallow fields and waste ground, and arable land. Declines of dragonflies have been particularly pronounced for fen vegetation. This same habitat was also associated with strong declines of grasshoppers, butterflies and molluscs. Grasshoppers and butterflies have also declined in dry heathlands. Butterflies, bumblebees and molluscs have declined in woodland edge, scrub and hedgerows. Macromoths have been lost from salt marsh, fallow fields and waste land. Dry heathland and fen species have undergone the most extensive declines. All the habitats we looked at have undergone losses of some major species groups.

This conclusion is supported by the analysis of population trends in British birds by the British Trust for Ornithology. It has shown substantial declines in numbers of many birds associated with farmland habitats from a variety of causes (Marchant *et al.* 1990). In some cases, food shortages are the problem. Finches, such as goldfinch (*Carduelis carduelis*) and linnet (*Carduelis cannabina*), have declined because of the loss of weedy winter stubbles, which provided food in the form of weed and crop seeds. Increased use of insecticides has reduced the abundance of *Dolerus* sawfly larvae and other insects in crops (Aebischer 1991), with consequent effects on their predators, including grey partridges (*Perdix perdix*) and skylarks (*Alauda arvensis*) (eg Potts 1991). In other cases, habitat loss has been the important factor. Not surprisingly, birds of damp grassland have become rarer as their habitats have been drained and modifed. Species such as snipe (*Gallinago gallinago*) and lapwing (*Vanellus vanellus*) from the fields themselves, and sedge warbler (*Acrocephalus schoenobaenus*) and grasshopper warbler (*Locustella naevia*) in hedges and scrub are all in decline. Birds of heathland, downland and other unintensive agricultural habitats have also declined as the habitat areas have been reduced. Some species need combinations of habitats; lapwings and stone curlews need short grass for feeding and longer grass for cover; similar combinations of cover also help owls, by providing hunting areas and places where their small mammal prey can thrive. Trends towards larger, more uniformly managed fields have made these habitat complexes less common.

Not all declines can be traced directly to changing farming practices. The swallow (*Hirundo rustica*) may have faced a shortage of insect food in some areas, but has also lost nest sites and has had to cope with drought in its African winter quarters. Also, not all farmland birds are decreasing: wintering geese populations are increasing to the point where they are becoming a serious pest, feeding on crops and grasslands near the coast, and some birds of prey (notably the sparrowhawk (*Accipter nisus*)) are recovering in numbers following the banning of persistent organochlorine pesticides.

Lessons for the management of set-aside land

The British countryside has become less rich in wildlife associated with farming for a variety of causes, but the loss of habitat diversity and of areas of traditional, low-input, managed habitat is a very important factor for many species. There is no single habitat which should be given top priority for restoration, no single species which should be of prime concern. Rather, set-aside should be used to replace some of the habitat diversity at local levels, and to help safeguard the continued existence of those rare habitats and rare species which remain on or nearby arable land. For example, set-aside can be managed to provide buffer areas near existing heath or species-rich grassland.

References

Aebischer, N.J. 1991. Twenty years of monitoring invertebrates and weeds in cereal fields in Sussex. In: *The ecology of temperate cereal fields*, edited by L.G. Firbank, N. Carter, J.F. Darbyshire & G.R. Potts, 305–331. Oxford : Blackwell Scientific.

Barr, C.J., Howard, D.C., Bunce, R.G.H., Gillespie, M.K. & Hallam, C.J. 1991. *Changes in hedgerows in Britain between 1984 and 1990.* (NERC contract report to Department of the Environment.) Grange-over-Sands: Institute of Terrestrial Ecology.

Batten, L.A., Bibby, C.J., Clement, P., Elliott, G.D. & Porter, R.F. 1990. *Red Data birds in Britain, action for rare, threatened and important species.* London: Poyser.

Bratton, J.H. 1991. *British Red Data Books 3: Invertebrates other than insects.* Peterborough: Joint Nature Conservation Committee.

Bunce, R.G.H., Barr, C.J. & Fuller, R.M. 1992. Integration of methods for detecting land use change, with special reference to Countryside Survey 1990. In: *Land use change: causes and consequences*, edited by M.C. Whitby, 69–78. (ITE symposium no. 27.) London: HMSO.

Bunce, R.G.H., Howard, D.C., Hallam, C.J., Barr, C.J. & Benefield, C.B. 1992. *The ecological consequences of land use change.* (NERC contract report to the Department of the Environment.) Grange-over-Sands: Institute of Terrestrial Ecology.

Commission of the European Communities. 1992. Council Directive 92/43/EEC of 21 May 1992 on the conservation of natural habitats and of wild fauna and flora. *Official Journal of the European Communities*, L 206, 7–50.

Firbank, L.G., Arnold, H.R., Eversham, B.C., Mountford, J.O., Radford, G.L., Telfer, M.G., Treweek, J.R., Webb, N.C.R. & Wells, T.C.E. 1992. *The potential uses of set-aside land to benefit wildlife* (NERC contract report to the Ministry of Agriculture, Fisheries and Food.) Abbots Ripton, Huntingdon: Institute of Terrestrial Ecology.

Fuller, R.M. 1987. The changing extent and conservation interest in lowland grasslands in England and Wales: a review of the grassland surveys 1930–84. *Biological Conservation*, **40**, 281–300.

Harding, P.T. & Sheail, J. 1992. The Biological Records Centre - a pioneer in data gathering and retrieval. In: *Biological recording of changes in British wildlife*, edited by P.T. Harding, 5–19. (ITE symposium no. 26.) London: HMSO.

Marchant, J.H., Hudson, R., Carter, S.P. & Whittington, P. 1990. *Population trends in British breeding birds.* Tring: British Trust for Ornithology.

Moore, N.W. 1962. The heaths of Dorset and their conservation. *Journal of Ecology*, **50**, 369–391.

Nature Conservancy Council. 1989. *Guidelines for the selection of biological SSSIs.* Peterborough: NCC.

Perring, F.H. & Farrell, L. 1977. *British Red Data Books 1: Vascular plants.* Nettleham: Royal Society for Nature Conservation.

Perring, F.H. & Farrell, L. 1983. *British Red Data Books 1: Vascular plants.* 2nd ed. Nettleham: Royal Society for Nature Conservation.

Potts, G.R. 1991. The environmental and ecological importance of cereal fields. In: *The ecology of temperate cereal fields*, edited by L.G. Firbank, N. Carter, J.F. Darbyshire & G.R. Potts, 3–21. Oxford: Blackwell Scientific.

Rackham, O. 1986. *The history of the countryside.* London: Dent.

Ratcliffe, D.A. 1984. Post-medieval and recent changes in British vegetation: the culmination of human influence. *New Phytologist,* **98**, 73–100.

Shirt, D.B. 1987. *British Red Data Books 2: Insects.* Peterborough: Nature Conservancy Council.

Webb, N.R. 1990. Changes on the heathlands of Dorset between 1978 and 1987. *Biological Conservation,* **51**, 273–286.

Webb, N.R. & Haskins, L.E. 1980. An ecological survey of heathlands in the Poole Basin, Dorset, England in 1978. *Biological Conservation,* **17**, 281–296.

3 WHAT CAN BE ACHIEVED ON SET-ASIDE FARMLAND?

Given time, money, energy and skill, and the right environmental conditions, habitats as diverse as salt marsh, forest, lowland heath, damp meadows, fen and upland grassland all have the potential to be restored on set-aside farmland. Even land left to regenerate naturally into untidy-looking fields full of weeds and volunteers and eventually into grassland, scrub and woodland can be very valuable to wildlife. However, not all set-aside is good for wildlife. It is possible to produce fields full of grass weeds of little benefit to wildlife and of concern to the farmer. Bird populations can be depleted by enticing them into apparently suitable areas of set-aside, only for their chicks to die following mis-timed mowing or cultivation.

Evidence that set-aside can be managed successfully for wildlife comes from the experimental Countryside Premium Scheme (Countryside Commission 1991). This is a programme in which farmers were given additional payments for managing land set-aside under the 1988 scheme for environmental benefit. Farmers were given a series of options (wooded margins, meadowland, Brent goose (*Branta bernicla bernicla*) pasture, wildlife fallow and habitat restoration), and applications were accepted at the discretion of the Countryside Commission. While the scheme as a whole appears to have met its general objective of an improved environment and greater capacity for quiet public recreation (Ewins & Roberts 1992), not all projects achieved their aims. For example, pastures for goose grazing were little used by the Brent geese when the sward height was allowed to exceed 9 cm (Vickery & Sutherland 1992), and a chalk grassland restoration project included a wide range of species from European and garden origin (Akeroyd 1992) and so failed to restore the local flora, although it was a successful creation of a pleasant public access area.

A particular success story for the management of set-aside comes from a Surrey farm which now accounts for over 6% of all birds ringed in England and Ireland (Rumsey 1989; Mead & Clark 1991). It was intensively cultivated as recently as 1985, with mature hedges and reed-filled ditches. A few fields have been set-aside each year with the intention of creating habitat for birds; drainage ditches have been dammed (without affecting other farms) and natural regeneration has been allowed from field boundaries and the seed bank. Only meadowsweet (*Filipendula ulmaria*) has been planted. The area now includes a complex of shallow lakes, reedbeds and scrub, and attracts a wide range of migrant and breeding species. This success has not come by accident; the farm was purchased with habitat creation in mind. The 1988 set-aside programme provided support, but not the initial incentive, and the hydrology and location were known to be suitable. Other farmers do not have the luxury of choosing a farm for a particular set-aside programme, and need to consider the possibilities and potential problems of their land before embarking upon their set-aside schemes.

Set-aside and plants

Plants arising on set-aside arable land originate from three main sources: seeds and plant fragments already present in the soil, seeds colonising from nearby or from more distant sources, and seeds or plants deliberately sown. Apart from the last case, it is difficult to generalise which species will appear on set-aside. They will depend on soil type, soil moisture, cropping history, past cultivation and herbicide practices, and other factors. However, they will frequently be crop volunteers and annual, weedy species in the first instance (Wilson 1992). This is not necessarily a problem from a conservation point of view, as some of our rarest plants may be represented, and even common broadleaved weeds will provide important food sources for insects, birds and small mammals. However, some fields may become dominated by grass weeds of concern to the farmer and little value to wildlife. They are typically on heavier soil with a history of intensive weed control.

On non-rotational set-aside, the plant community will become dominated by perennial plants, which again depend on what species are present or can invade from nearby sources (Wilson 1992). Natural colonisation by the less usual species from distant sources is unlikely. The management regime is also critical; the choice of grazing and cutting regimes can have profound effects on the development of the community (eg Tansley 1939; Bakker 1989); further details are given under the different management options.

Conservation for scarce plants on set-aside land is most likely to be profitable in arable fields with existing populations of rare weeds, where the field boundaries are old and have not been managed intensively, and in long-term habitat recreation of grassland and heath either adjacent to existing land or in areas only recently transformed into arable or intensive grazing. Habitat restoration in other areas will benefit some of the more widespread species of grasslands and hedgerows, depending on local conditions and propagule sources.

Set-aside and invertebrates

Heathland, grassland, field water and woodland margins have all witnessed declines in at least some groups of invertebrates. The declines on arable land have been attested to elsewhere (Potts 1991), and can be attributed to changing land management and increased levels of pesticides. The emphasis for insect conservation on set-aside land has to be on increasing habitat diversity. One could manage set-aside field boundaries for insects which benefit the cropped area. For example, bumblebees, important for crop pollination, have declined particularly in hedgerow and water fringe vegetation. They tend to prefer to visit perennial species (Fussell & Corbet 1992), which can be encouraged at the bottom of hedges under set-aside. Field margins can also be managed to increase natural enemies of aphids, including hoverflies and carabid beetles (Wratten & Powell 1991), which may reduce the need for insecticides within the cropped areas. Butterflies, especially skippers and browns, can be encouraged by ensuring that there is a range of wildflowers in the field and field margin that overlap in flowering time, giving continuous sources of nectar.

In general, summer cutting reduces invertebrate populations and temporarily removes nectar sources. However, if the cutting is rotated around the field, the overall flowering period can actually be extended, and a mosaic of habitats can be created which will increase the diversity of species.

Our analysis of species declines revealed major losses of invertebrates from water margin vegetation and from lowland heaths. Restoration of ponds, ditches and slow-moving rivers and their associated vegetation may help to reverse the declines of species such as the variable damselfly (*Coenagrion pulchellum*), which has disappeared from many localities in eastern England because of drainage and vegetation clearance. Habitat loss has also been responsible for losses of characteristic lowland heath species, such as the grayling (*Hipparchia semele*) and silver-studded blue (*Plebejus argus*) butterflies.

Set-aside and terrestrial vertebrates

The conservation potential of set-aside for birds is great because:

- recent declines in numbers of typical farmland birds can be slowed or reversed by providing new habitats;
- there is increasing knowledge about the management for birds of farmland in general (Lack 1992) and of set-aside in particular (Osborne 1989; Game Conservancy 1992);
- many species are highly mobile and so can colonise new habitats.

Many species should benefit from general measures, such as the increased availability of winter stubbles and invertebrate-rich grasslands. Surveys on land set-aside in 1988 appear to confirm this view, with even the rare cirl bunting (*Emberiza cirlus*) increasing in numbers on and around set-aside land (Sears 1992). Some species require more specific measures, however. In England, the dark-bellied Brent goose and the stone curlew (*Burhinus oedicnemus*) require specific management and targeting for winter feeding and summer breeding areas, respectively.

There has been less work on mammals on set-aside than on birds.

However, it is likely that arable wood mice (*Apodemus sylvaticus*) will take advantage of the insect-rich conditions expected on uncut first-year natural regeneration (see Tew, Macdonald & Rands 1992), but in subsequent years voles would exploit the more dense canopy conditions (eg Rogers 1992). Rabbits (*Oryctolagus cuniculus*) may become very numerous on set-aside land. Rarer mammals such as the brown hare (*Lepus europaeus*) would be expected to benefit from natural regeneration set-aside programmes, and bats may take advantage of increased supplies of insects, provided suitable roosts are available. The otter (*Lutra lutra*) is one example of a mammal that needs specific management which could be carried out on set-aside land.

The more widespread amphibians – common frog (*Rana temporaria*), common toad (*Bufo bufo*), smooth newt (*Triturus vulgaris*), palmate newt (*Triturus helveticus*) and great crested newt (*Triturus cristatus*) – could potentially benefit from the creation of ponds on set-aside land, although natural colonisation depends on populations existing nearby. Ponds may also benefit grass snakes (*Natrix natrix*), and a less tidy and less disturbed landscape will tend to favour this species and our other widely distributed reptiles – adder (*Vipera berus*), common lizard (*Lacerta vivipara*) and slow worm (*Anguis fragilis*). The smooth snake (*Coronella austriaca*), sand lizard (*Lacerta agilis*) and natterjack toad (*Bufo calamita*) could benefit from lowland heath restoration.

Lessons for the management of set-aside land

A substantial range of wildlife has been observed on land set-aside under the 1988 scheme (Clarke 1992). Land management targeted for wildlife may be expected to be even richer in species. Management should aim to make the best use of the wildlife already present or capable of reaching the site. This implies that a variety of management options should be available to farmers, who can then select those appropriate to the local conditions. This selection is not a trivial task, and implies a detailed knowledge of the present, past and potential habitats on the farm, as well as an appreciation of what can be achieved, what cannot be achieved, and the limits of our knowledge of farming for wildlife. The farmer needs to have advice ready to hand, especially for the more complex forms of management; the Countryside Commission found it spent six times as long advising farmers on the habitat restoration option of the Countryside Premium Scheme than the other options.

It must be stressed that set-aside can be very harmful to wildlife. In the USA, populations of game birds actually fell during a set-aside programme. Breeding birds were encouraged on to set-aside land early in the season, only for their broods to be destroyed by the early cutting of the set-aside cover (Sotherton, Boatman & Robertson 1992). The rotational set-aside scheme had similar effects for ground-nesting birds and other wildlife in the spring of 1993. The revised rules for 1993–94 address this problem by allowing farmers to delay cutting and cultivation until mid-summer.

References

Akeroyd, J. 1992. A remarkable alien flora on the Gog Magog Hills. *Nature in Cambridgeshire*, **34**, 35–42.

Bakker, J.P. 1989. *Nature management by grazing and cutting.* Dordrecht: Kluwer.

Clarke, J., ed. 1992. *Set-aside.* Farnham: British Crop Protection Council.

Countryside Commission. 1991. *The countryside premium for set-aside land.* Cambridge: Countryside Commission.

Ewins, A.E. & Roberts, R.J. 1992. The countryside premium scheme for set-aside land. In: *Set-aside*, edited by J. Clarke, 229–234. Farnham: British Crop Protection Council.

Fussell, M. & Corbet, S.A. 1992. Flower use by bumble-bees: a basis for forage plant management. *Journal of Applied Ecology*, **29**, 451–465.

Game Conservancy. 1992. *Management of rotational set-aside for game.* (Factsheet no. 2.) Fordingbridge: Game Conservancy

Lack, P. 1992. *Birds on lowland farms.* London: HMSO.

Mead, C.J. & Clark, J.A. 1991. Report on bird ringing for Britain and Ireland for 1990. *Ringing and Migration*, **12**, 139–176.

Osborne, P. 1989. *The management of set-aside land for birds: a practical guide.* Sandy: Royal Society for the Protection of Birds.

Potts, G.R. 1991. The environmental and ecological importance of cereal fields. In: *The ecology of temperate cereal fields,* edited by L.G. Firbank, N. Carter, J.F. Darbyshire & G.R. Potts, 3–21. Oxford : Blackwell Scientific.

Rogers, L.N. 1992. The ecology of small mammals on set-aside agricultural land. In: *Set-aside,* edited by J. Clarke, 201–202. Farnham: British Crop Protection Council.

Rumsey, S.J.R. 1989. Creating a new ringing site from farmland. *BTO Ringers' Bulletin,* **7,** 76.

Sears, J. 1992. The value of set-aside to birds. In: *Set-aside,* edited by J. Clarke, 175–180. Farnham: British Crop Protection Council.

Sotherton, N.W., Boatman, N.D. & Robertson, P.A. 1992. The use of set-aside land for game conservation. In: *Set-aside,* edited by J. Clarke, 223–228. Farnham: British Crop Protection Council.

Tansley, A.G. 1939. *The British Islands and their vegetation.* Cambridge: Cambridge University Press.

Tew, T.E., Macdonald, D.W. & Rands, M.R.W. 1992. Herbicide application affects microhabitat use by arable wood mice (*Apodemus sylvaticus*). *Journal of Applied Ecology,* **29,** 532–539.

Vickery, J.A. & Sutherland, W.J. 1992. Brent geese: a conflict between conservation and agriculture. In: *Set-aside,* edited by J. Clarke, 187–193. Farnham: British Crop Protection Council.

Wilson, P.J. 1992. The natural regeneration of vegetation under set-aside in southern England. In: *Set-aside,* edited by J. Clarke, 73–78. Farnham: British Crop Protection Council.

Wratten, S.D. & Powell, W. 1991. Cereal aphids and their natural enemies. In: *The ecology of temperate cereal fields,* edited by L.G. Firbank, N. Carter, J.F. Darbyshire & G.R. Potts, 233–257. Oxford: Blackwell Scientific.

4 A RANGE OF SET-ASIDE MANAGEMENT OPTIONS

In order to achieve a greater diversity of habitat, there must be a variety of ways of managing set-aside land. The rules for the set-aside and habitat schemes allow for considerable flexibility, which can be increased still further by devising particular management programmes to suit local conditions.

The options we cover in this book are as follows.

Rotational set-aside

Management for rare arable weeds
Management for birds

Non-rotational set-aside

A field margin scheme for hedges, wooded and aquatic boundaries
Otter havens
Management of natural regeneration and sown cover
Brent goose pasture
Stone curlew meadow

Longer-term habitat restoration

Restoration of chalk grassland
Restoration of lowland damp grassland
Restoration of heath and sandy grassland
Restoration of salt marsh

There is a degree of overlap between these options; for example, natural regeneration may lead to the development of damp grassland in some areas, and a habitat established under non-rotational set-aside may be suitable for transfer to the Habitat Scheme.

General principles of scheme selection by farmers

At a given site, there will be several options available to the farmer, depending on the rules of the set-aside programmes. From the point of view of conservation of species and habitats, however, some options will be more valuable than others on particular sites.

The first question relates to the presence of rare species and habitats now. If there are Brent geese (*Branta bernicla bernicla*), stone curlews (*Burhinus oedicnemus*) or otters (*Lutra lutra*) on or near the land, then the options for these species should be considered first. If there are rare arable weeds, then the rotational set-aside should be considered for use with permanent Conservation Headlands (Game Conservancy 1992).

If the site is, has been, or is adjacent to lowland heath, damp grassland, chalk grassland or salt marsh, then restoration of these habitats should be considered. The most important indicators of potential success of habitat restoration are evidence that the habitat is found on that site now, or that it has been present in the past and remains in close proximity to the site. The first proves that the habitat is compatible with the site, the second that a pool of species is available to colonise the habitat. The less time which has elapsed since the onset of arable farming, and the less distance to the species pool, the better.

Field margin set-aside should be considered wherever there are drainage ditches, woodlands and hedgerows with diverse flora already present. The desired degree of ingress of the marginal vegetation itself (as scrub or young woodland) should be considered.

For many fields, there are substantial benefits to wildlife by allowing natural regeneration or sowing suitable green cover. These benefits are relatively quick to achieve, and the land can be readily returned to productive agriculture.

Finally, the farmer should consider enhancing the benefits of the set-aside to wildlife by providing nest and roost boxes, creating ponds, and by controlling access by machines and people if necessary.

In all cases, the farmer should develop a whole-farm plan for environmental set-aside, ideally in consultation with a visiting advisor. Set-aside is best used to enhance what already exists, and so both farmer and advisor should be aware of rare and declining species and valuable habitats on the farm. The plan should also take account of any other environmental schemes available or already adopted that can complement the set-aside work; these include Environmentally Sensitive Areas, Nitrate Sensitive Areas, Countryside Stewardship Scheme, Hedgerow Incentive Scheme and others. It should also acknowledge other legal or contractual constraints, such as responsibility to the local water authority to maintain watercourses.

An assessment framework for set-aside schemes

An assessment framework is required to help identify suitable areas for the restoration of the selected habitat types and selected species, to define appropriate management strategies on chosen sites, and to monitor the success of set-aside options in achieving habitat restoration on those sites. There may also be off-site implications of the management needed to restore habitats on set-aside land.

For each target habitat, the following are therefore provided:

- criteria for site selection
- predicted implications of different management options on selected sites
- criteria for appraising selected sites/management options
- information to predict off-site impacts.

Criteria for site selection

The successful restoration of habitats depends on a number of factors, including:

- physical characteristics of sites (geology, soil, climate, topography, size)

- locational attributes (proximity to existing 'good' habitat, location within surrounding landscape matrix, etc)
- management history
- restorability of habitat with current techniques
- time and money available for restoration.

For each habitat type, the ranges of acceptability for the selection criteria will vary. Where detailed information is available, it is included. For example, some habitats have quite specific soil requirements, or support associated species which have very limited dispersal ability, thereby restricting the availability of suitable sites. Also, in some cases the suitability of a site can be chosen on the basis of simple, national rules which can be administered centrally, while in other cases suitability is best assessed at a more local level and national rules are inappropriate. Note is taken where an option might overlap with national environmental schemes.

Management

The aim is to define appropriate management for each habitat. Potentially damaging operations are noted (including those which might operate on adjacent land). Where appropriate, reclamation and maintenance management are distinguished. Any site preparation techniques (nutrient stripping, etc) which improve the chances of success are noted.

An indication is given of the likely timescales required for habitat restoration to be successful.

Financial and management inputs are likely to be higher for some habitats, and for some management options, than for others. Whilst we do not provide costings, indications of the nature of expenditure or savings are provided.

We have attempted to produce summary information suitable for managing the habitats as wholes. More specialist literature should also be consulted where necessary; for example, those interested in bird conservation should consult Lack (1992) and Osborne (1989). We have not attempted complete literature reviews.

Appraisal

Criteria for judging the success, or otherwise, of habitat restoration on set aside-land are required to ensure that the land has been managed appropriately and also to feed back information to refine management prescriptions. They may include:

- reductions in soil nutrient availability
- achievement of appropriate hydrological conditions
- species richness
- presence of 'indicator' or characteristic species and communities
- absence of all-engulfing, aggressive weeds
- habitat structure, eg scrub/grassland mosaic.

These criteria should be compatible with the 'aim' for each target habitat. For example, if the aim is to restore an arable site in Dorset to lowland dry heathland within ten years with a representative range of associated species present, the assessment criteria to be applied after ten years would include the presence of plants representative of lowland dry heathland in Dorset. However, some aims are less easily assessed; for example, if the aim is to increase numbers of seed-eating birds, simple counts within a field may be distorted by the mobility and visibility of the birds. In this case, a broader-scale census may be more appropriate. Also, important gains may be made even though the primary objective is not achieved; for example, set-aside river banks which are unsuccessful in attracting otters may benefit other wildlife such as kingfishers (*Alcedo atthis*), and an attempt to recreate a species-rich grassland may produce a less diverse sward that becomes valued as an area for public access.

One approach is to install a hierarchy of monitoring systems:

- national changes, based on ongoing monitoring schemes such as the Butterfly Monitoring Scheme of the Biological Records Centre (Pollard & Yates 1993);

- landscape changes, using land cover mapping from air or satellite to record gross levels of landscape structure;

- species and communities on individual sites through time.

Monitoring of species and communities needs to take into account all targeted groups, and not simply plants. In particular, the National Vegetation Classification (NVC) (Rodwell 1991, 1992) should not be the sole basis for monitoring, as:

- set-aside communities are unlikely to accord with a classification designed for semi-natural communities – restored habitats are likely to contain a balance of arable and introduced species for many years;

- plants are likely to respond to management changes less rapidly and consistently than more mobile groups, such as birds;

- habitat structure is ignored.

The guidelines for selecting biological Sites of Special Scientific Interest (SSSIs) (Nature Conservancy Council 1989) offer a more rounded model for appraisal. We have not attempted to provide comprehensive criteria for appraisal, but we have suggested approaches which could be included as part of an appraisal programme.

Potential off-site impacts

These relate primarily to potential pest and weed problems. For example, restoration of salt marsh might encourage flocks of geese which can inflict considerable damage on neighbouring crops. Impacts can also be beneficial, eg reductions in nitrogen runoff, increased numbers of beneficial insect predators, etc. We suggest ways in which appropriate management might reduce or remove adverse impacts.

Implications for access

If access should be controlled or denied, this is stated.

References

Game Conservancy. 1992. *Guidelines 1992/93: Management of Conservation Headlands.* Fordingbridge: Game Conservancy.

Lack, P. 1992. *Birds on lowland farms.* London: HMSO.

Nature Conservancy Council. 1989. *Guidelines for the selection of biological SSSIs.* Peterborough: NCC.

Osborne, P. 1989. *The management of set-aside land for birds: a practical guide.* Sandy: Royal Society for the Protection of Birds.

Pollard, E. & Yates, T.J. 1993. *Monitoring butterflies for ecology and conservation.* London: Chapman & Hall.

Rodwell, J.S. 1991, 1992. *British plant communities, vols 1-5.* Cambridge: Joint Nature Conservancy Council/Cambridge University Press.

ROTATIONAL SET-ASIDE

5 ROTATIONAL SET-ASIDE FOR RARE ARABLE WEEDS AND BIRDS

Summary

Rare arable weeds can be found on many soils and in many areas, but are most common on light soils in the south and east of England. They should be managed by light cultivation at a time of year appropriate for the particular species, and populations should be maintained between set-aside years by using Conservation Headlands. Rotational set-aside can be used to benefit seed-eating and insectivorous birds by allowing natural regeneration without cutting; insectivorous and game birds by sowing cereal-based cover; insectivorous birds and birds of prey by minimally cultivating part of the field in early spring.

First-year and rotational set-aside can support a wide range of plants and animals, including rarities and species which have declined because of changes in farm practices.

The 1993 rules allow considerable flexibility, giving farmers the opportunity to manage the land for the benefit of some of our rarest plants and some of our best-known birds. To this end, green cover should usually be established by natural regeneration, and managed as late as possible before the deadlines for cutting (before 15 August) and destruction (31 August). Earlier weed control is allowed by cultivation in May and even earlier by herbicides and cutting, but the costs to wildlife can be severe. Rare plants will not have set seeds, and birds will not have fledged their chicks.

Rotational set-aside for rare arable weeds

Introduction

Our arable weed communities have changed dramatically over the last century, so that many of the traditional sights of cereal farming, such as cornflower (*Centaurea cyanus*) and corn cockle (*Agrostemma githago*), are now very rare or even extinct in Britain. There is no single factor to blame; improved seed cleaning, herbicide use, trends towards early autumn sowing, and increased levels of nutrients have all contributed to increases in grass weeds and reductions in the 'traditional' broadleaved weed floras (Svensson & Wigren 1986; Wilson 1991). Many remaining populations of rare weeds survive in field margins and in the seed banks. Some of these have flourished in Conservation Headlands, which are strips around the edge of field subject to restricted pesticide and herbicide use (Sotherton 1991), and over 240 species of plant have been recorded in first-year set-aside (Andrews 1992). These experiences prove that well-managed set-aside land can benefit at least some of these rare plants.

Two general approaches are possible; one may manage populations already in existence, and one may create new weed floras by sowing. Here, we concentrate on the first option, which assumes that the farmer knows which species are present on the land. Much of the following account is adapted from Wilson's (1991) study of the biology and conservation of rare arable weeds.

Criteria for site selection

The ideal site will have a history of at least one species of rare arable weed, although some species may have been restricted to the seed bank for many years, or may not have been noticed. Also, the farmer may wish to sow desired species. The soil is likely to be light and sandy or chalky, but most soils support some rare species.

Information necessary to identify and define suitable sites

Target habitat	Arable, for rare weeds.
Location of site	Anywhere.
Location of site in relation to target habitat distribution	Not applicable.

Information necessary to assess the suitability of the site for restoration to the target habitat type

Many sites will be unsuitable, as management for weeds will favour noxious species, rather than desirable rare species.

Size	Any.
Soils	Soils are typically (but not exclusively) light, sandy or chalky and well drained. Soil fertility should ideally be low.
Recent management history	The land will have a long history of arable use. Recent management is not critical, although ideally herbicide and fertilizer inputs should have been low.
Management on adjacent land	Not applicable.
Proximity to existing habitat	Not applicable – it is assumed that recruitment will come from the seed bank.

Checklist of additional features

None.

Other designations/schemes

Compatible with Environmentally Sensitive Areas, and, in a small number of cases, with SSSI management and wildlife enhancement schemes.

Management

Allow natural regeneration after harvesting the previous crop. Then, minimally cultivate the soil (to a depth of not more than 6–7 cm) between 10 October and 10 November. Cutting should be delayed for as long as possible, certainly until August. Application of selective herbicides against problem weeds is allowed, but they should be used with caution; the Game Conservancy's list of selective herbicides is a useful guide (Game Conservancy 1992a).

Different species require different timing of tillage, and Forche (1991) recorded an increase in some rare arable weeds in the absence of tillage. The farmer can decide not to till, or to apply for permission to adopt a light March tillage, depending on the range of species present.

If weed populations are to be sown, then seeds should be of British (ideally local) provenance, and sown to densities of around 5–25 plants m^{-2} of each species into a prepared seed bed; fertilizers are not required (Svensson & Wigren 1986). The seeds may be planted in the outer 6 m of the field only, to take advantage of Conservation Headlands in subsequent crops. Local floras should be consulted as to appropriate species mixtures; guidance should also be obtained from a competent body.

Aim of management
To allow the build up of seed reserves of rare arable weeds.

Site preparation techniques (if any)
None is required, unless planting seeds, in which case minimum cultivation should be performed before planting.

Options for follow-up management
Continued use and high levels of nitrates will eliminate many of the benefits of the set-aside year. Therefore, succeeding crops should incorporate Conservation Headlands (Sotherton 1991) managed according to the latest guidelines of the Game Conservancy (Game Conservancy 1992a), thus taking advantage of the tendency of rare weeds to be concentrated around the field margin (Wilson 1989), or those guidelines should be applied across the whole field until the next set-aside. Fertilizer inputs should ideally be low.

Financial implications (capital and recurrent costs)
None, except the costs of seeds and herbicides, if required.

Potential off-site implications of different options
Reduced fertilizer and pesticide runoff. Volunteer cereals have the potential to act as sources of disease infection (Thresh 1981), but the risks appear to be small in practice (Yarham & Symonds 1992).

Procedures and problems encountered for return to arable land

There may be some build-up of noxious weeds, especially annual grasses and couch-grass (*Elymus repens*) (Shield & Godwin 1992). However, fields should not be managed in this way where such weeds are already abundant. Weed control can be enhanced by following the set-aside with a break crop.

Additional on-site implications for management

The winter stubbles will provide food for many birds. Game birds will benefit.

Timescales

Not applicable.

Potentially damaging operations

These include the application of fertilizer and broad-spectrum herbicides at any time, except for spot application of herbicide, and cultivation and cutting before early August.

Appraisal

If successful, the field should contain one or more rare or uncommon weeds (Table 1 provides a guide list) in the current and in future seasons.

Potential off-site impacts

None.

Implications for access

None.

Table 1. Uncommon arable weeds within Britain. Values refer to the number of records since 1970 (data from Biological Records Centre, ITE)

Common name	Latin name

Rare (found in fewer than 15 10 km squares)

Pheasant's eye	*Adonis annua*
Blue pimpernel	*Anagallis arvensis foemina*
Broadleaved cudweed	*Filago pyramidata*
Western fumitory	*Fumaria occidentalis*
Rough corn bedstraw	*Galium tricornutum*
Broad-fruited corn salad	*Valerianella rimosa*

Scarce (found in between 16 and 100 10 km squares)

Loose-flowered silky bent	*Apera spica-venti*
Lesser quaking grass	*Briza minor*
Small-flowered fumitory	*Fumaria parviflora*
Vaillants fumitory	*Fumaria vaillantii*
Corn caraway	*Petroselinum segetum*
Small-flowered catchfly	*Silene gallica*
Spreading hedge-parsley	*Torilis arvensis*
Slender tare	*Vicia tenuissima*

Uncommon (found in over 100 10 km squares)

Fig-leaved goosefoot	*Chenopodium ficifolium*
Corn marigold	*Chrysanthemum segetum*
Broad spurge	*Euphorbia platyphyllos*
Dense-flowered fumitory	*Fumaria densiflora*
Narrow-leaved hemp-nettle	*Galeopsis angustifolia*
Long-stalked cranesbill	*Geranium columbinum*
Sharp-leaved fluellen	*Kickxia elatine*
Round-leaved fluellen	*Kickxia spuria*
Corn gromwell	*Lithospermum arvense*
Lesser snapdragon	*Misopates orontium*
Mousetail	*Myosurus minimus*
Long prickly-headed poppy	*Papaver argemone*
Rough prickly-headed poppy	*Papaver hybridum*
Corn crowfoot	*Ranunculus arvensis*
Small-flowered buttercup	*Ranunculus parviflorus*
Shepherd's needle	*Scandix pecten-veneris*
Night-flowering campion	*Silene noctiflora*
Field woundwort	*Stachys arvensis*
Green field speedwell	*Veronica agrestis*

Rotational set-aside for birds

Introduction

Birds associated with arable land have declined because of shortages of food (seeds for wintering finches, insects for skylarks (*Alauda arvensis*) and gamebirds), destruction of nests and nestlings by management, and shortage of the required combinations of habitat structure (O'Connor & Shrubb 1986; Lack 1992). These problems can be alleviated on set-aside land with proper management (Osborne 1989): surveys have shown that naturally regenerated set-aside, and set-aside managed as wildlife fallow (*sensu* Countryside Commission 1991, see below) and as meadowland (*sensu* Countryside Commission 1991) appear to attract greater numbers of birds than adjacent arable areas (Sears 1992).

Seed eaters (eg finches), insectivores (eg game, skylarks), birds of prey (eg kestrels (*Falco tinnunculus*), owls) and carrion eaters (eg rooks (*Corvus frugilegus*)) may benefit from properly managed rotational set-aside. For example, set-aside in south Devon may reverse the near-extinction of the cirl bunting (*Emberiza cirlus*), by providing feeding areas rich in broadleaved weeds close to the nesting sites of large, untrimmed hedges and scrub (A Evans, pers. comm.).

The rules for rotational set-aside may benefit wintering seed eaters and some insectivores by providing winter cereal cover crops for game birds. However, experience from studies of game birds in the USA suggests that cutting naturally regenerating land in the spring and early summer kills chicks directly or exposes them to predation (Sotherton, Boatman & Robertson 1992). Cutting large areas simultaneously gives short-term benefit to birds of prey and carrion eaters, but otherwise is damaging for birds.

In this section, we consider different management strategies designed to favour different groups of bird species. They depend upon either allowing natural regeneration or sowing different kinds of cover.

Criteria for site selection

Information necessary to identify and define suitable sites

Target habitat   Fallow.

Location of site   Not applicable.

Location of site in   Not applicable.
relation to target
habitat distribution

Information necessary to assess the suitability of the site for restoration to the target habitat type
Not applicable.

Checklist of additional features
None.

Other designations/schemes
Compatible with Environmentally Sensitive Areas.

Management

For seed eating birds
Do nothing between harvesting the crop before set-aside and cutting and cultivation, which should be delayed until August.

For insectivorous birds
Either:
- do nothing between harvesting the crop before set-aside and cutting and cultivation, which should be delayed until August;

or
- sow a cereal and brassica mixture in the autumn or undersow into the previous crop to provide winter cover and food for game birds (Game Conservancy 1992b; Sotherton *et al.* 1992);

or
- minimally cultivate or plough the winter stubble in March (exemption required) and sow with a spring mixture (eg spring

oats, rye, sunflowers, spring rape and mustard) to provide brood-rearing habitat for game and other birds.

For insectivorous birds and birds of prey

Lightly cultivate (exemption required) or cut part of the winter stubble area in March to provide the required mosaic of habitats for ground-nesting birds such as lapwing (*Vanellus vanellus*), while providing open hunting areas for birds of prey.

Spot treatments of selective herbicides may be considered.

Aim of management
To boost numbers of birds.

Site preparation techniques (if any)
None required.

Options for follow-up management
Seed eaters and insectivores rely on the presence of broadleaved weeds within the crop environment. The use of Conservation Headlands (Sotherton 1991), or the application of the rules of Conservation Headlands (Game Conservancy 1992a) across the whole area will ensure the continued presence of these plants, improving their value to wildlife during the whole cropping and set-aside rotation.

Financial implications (capital and recurrent costs)
None.

Potential off-site implications of different options
There are risks of disease and insect pest spread from volunteer cereals to adjacent crops, but these appear to be slight (eg Yarham & Symonds 1992).

Procedures and problems encountered for return to arable land
There may be some build-up of noxious weeds, especially annual grasses and couch-grass (Shield & Godwin 1992); cereal/brassica mixtures would provide weed control. Disease and pest problems in future crops seem to be minor (Yarham & Symonds 1992).

Additional on-site implications for management

Rare weeds and small mammals will benefit from the uncut treatments; some rare weeds will benefit from the summer-cultivated treatments.

Timescales

Not applicable.

Potentially damaging operations

Cutting or cultivating the whole field between 31 March and 31 July.

Appraisal

There should be a greater number of individuals and of species of birds than in adjacent arable land. Numbers are not easy to assess, given the mobility of birds, their different seasonal uses of land, and different degrees of visibility in different habitats.

Potential off-site impacts

None.

Implications for access

The site should not be greatly disturbed during April–July, but a low level of casual walkers would be quite acceptable.

References

Andrews, J. 1992. Some practical problems in set-aside management for wildlife. *British Wildlife*, **3**, 329–336.

Countryside Commission. 1991. *The countryside premium for set-aside land.* Cambridge: Countryside Commission.

Forche, T. 1991. Changing vegetation and weed floras during set-aside and afterwards. In: *Brighton Crop Protection Conference Weeds – 1991*, 377–386. Farnham: British Crop Protection Council.

Game Conservancy. 1992a. *Guidelines 1992/93: management of Conservation Headlands.* Fordingbridge: Game Conservancy.

Game Conservancy. 1992b. *Management of rotational set-aside for game.* (Factsheet no. 2.) Fordingbridge: Game Conservancy.

Lack, P. 1992. *Birds on lowland farms.* London: HMSO.

O'Connor, R.J. & Shrubb, M. 1986. *Farming and birds.* Cambridge: Cambridge University Press.

Osborne, P. 1989. *The management of set-aside land for birds: a practical guide.* Sandy: Royal Society for the Protection of Birds.

Sears, J. 1992. The value of set-aside to birds. In: *Set-aside,* edited by J. Clarke, 175–180. Farnham: British Crop Protection Council.

Shield, I.F. & Godwin, R.J. 1992. Changes in species composition of a natural regeneration sward during the five year set-aside scheme. In: *Set-aside,* edited by J. Clarke, 123–128. Farnham: British Crop Protection Council.

Sotherton, N.W. 1991. Conservation Headlands: a practical combination of intensive cereal farming and conservation. In: *The ecology of temperate cereal fields,* edited by L.G. Firbank, N. Carter, J.F. Darbyshire & G.R. Potts, 373–397. Oxford: Blackwell Scientific.

Sotherton, N.W., Boatman, N.D. & Robertson, P.A. 1992. The use of set-aside land for game conservation. In: *Set-aside,* edited by J. Clarke, 223–228. Farnham: British Crop Protection Council.

Svensson, R. & Wigren, M. 1986. A survey of the history, biology and preservation of some retreating synanthropic plants. *Acta Universitatis Upsaliensis: Symbolae Botanicae Upsaliensis,* **25**, 4.

Thresh, J.M. 1981. The role of weeds and wild plants in the epidemiology of plant virus diseases. In: *Pests, pathogens and vegetation,* edited by J.M. Thresh, 53–70. London: Pitman.

Wilson, P.J. 1989. The distribution of arable weed seedbanks and the implications for the conservation of endangered species and communities. In: *Brighton Crop Protection Conference – Weeds 1989,* 1081–1086. Farnham: British Crop Protection Council.

Wilson, P.J. 1991. *The ecology and conservation of rare arable weed species.* PhD thesis, University of Southampton.

Yarham, D.J. & Symonds, B.V. 1992. Effects of set-aside on diseases of cereals. In: *Set-aside,* edited by J. Clarke, 41–46. Farnham: British Crop Protection Council.

NON-ROTATIONAL SET-ASIDE

Non-rotational set-aside involves an agreement to keep the same land in set-aside for at least five years (although there are a few exceptions). This agreement allows for the restoration of a greater variety of habitats than is possible under rotational set-aside, and allows a build-up of local populations of plants and animals, and so is, in general, better for wildlife.

The rules for set-aside apply for the whole period, although the cover can be put to limited agricultural use between 1 September and 14 January. This allows a limited degree of grazing. Particularly attractive land may be entered into the proposed Countryside Access Scheme, due to be introduced in 1994.

There are four basic options: field margins and strips, grassland, natural regeneration, and wild bird cover, although other management programmes are also provided for. In general, these options are intended to benefit a broad range of species by increasing the overall diversity of habitats within the countryside. However, there are a few notable species which have habitat requirements that can readily be created using set-aside, which have high conservation importance, and which are associated with farmland habitats. Brent geese (*Branta bernicla bernicla*) have a high international importance, but can achieve pest proportions locally; set-aside can be used to provide feeding areas for these birds which they will prefer to crops. The stone curlew (*Burhinus oedicnemus*) is a rare bird which breeds in large, open areas which can readily be maintained using set-aside. And while the otter (*Lutra lutra*) has many needs which cannot be met by set-aside alone, such as lack of disturbance and clean rivers, set-aside river banks can be used to provide much-needed holt sites for situations otherwise suitable for this rare and fascinating mammal. Other species can also be given special consideration by drawing up management plans in conjunction with an advisory organisation.

6 SET-ASIDE FOR FIELD MARGINS

Summary

The simple act of allowing ditch vegetation to grow will support a wide range of invertebrates and birds. More complex management of water tables and the creation of larger areas of water fringe vegetation will bring even greater benefits. Hedges are valuable for many birds, insects and plants; they also form an historical document of our landscape. Rotational management of hedges maintains a diversity of habitat structure and food items. Hedges should often be allowed to grow quite large, and sometimes to extend to become scrub areas. A sown or naturally regenerated strip of grass and wild flowers between the arable area of the field and the field margin can act as a buffer zone, provide access for farmers and walkers, boost numbers of beneficial insects, and attract birds and butterflies.

There have been substantial losses of species from the field margin habitats of water margin, hedgerow, and woodland edge. These habitats can be restored by putting down field margins to non-rotational set-aside, which would also provide opportunities to establish grassland, ponds and other habitats.

There are agronomic benefits in setting aside field margins, as yields are lower than in the centre of the field, and field margins can be used to facilitate access by machinery. Bumblebees and valuable insect predators such as hoverflies can be promoted. Environmental benefits include reducing the leaching of fertilizers and pollutants from remaining cropped areas into surface waters, as well as the creation and enhancement of public access.

The benefits to wildlife are three-fold:

* suitable habitats are created for a wide range of species;
* existing wildlife in field boundaries can be enhanced and protected from agricultural activity by buffer areas; and

- systems of corridors are created for some species, linking systems of wood or water bodies to facilitate colonisation of new habitats and recovery from extinction within existing habitats (Bunce & Howard 1990).

Field boundary habitats are potentially very rich, as they may provide conditions suitable for species of grassland, shrub, woodland edge and water fringe habitats within close proximity. The costs to wildlife would occur largely through the loss of any rare weeds at the edges of currently cropped areas.

The 1992 rules for both rotational and non-rotational set-aside allow for field margins, as long as they are at least 20 m wide throughout, and cover an area of at least 0.3 ha. Strips within the field are allowed. Field boundaries were also included in the 1988 five-year set-aside scheme.

Such wide margins should be structured as a series of habitats moving in to the field centre, from the woodland, hedge or water boundary, through tall herb vegetation, to a grassed area leading up to the boundary of the cropped area. The sequence can be continued by providing Conservation Headlands for maximum benefit to wildlife; bare strips around the cropped area are used by predatory beetles and can be a useful feeding area for birds (Lack 1992; see also Deane 1989). Management should aim to improve on features already present, as well as to create new ones.

In this section, three elements of the field margin will be treated separately:

- drainage ditches
- woodland edge and hedgerow
- meadow strips between the boundary and the cropped area.

The grassed area need not be the widest, as the boundary vegetation can be extended into the set-aside area by allowing scrub or reedbed development. Additionally, the nature of the boundary need not be uniform around the field; for example, three sides could have set-aside field margins, while the fourth could have a Conservation Headland adjacent to the hedge to benefit game chicks, which cannot penetrate dense grass (Sotherton, Boatman & Robertson 1992). Also, set-aside features may run across the fields, forming either new field boundaries or grassland strips.

This section does not deal with field margins bordering rivers and streams, where there are opportunities for conserving otters (*Lutra lutra*); such areas are dealt with in the following chapter. Also, it should be noted that the management option of encouraging reeds alongside ditches can be readily adapted to allow the creation of substantial reedbeds.

Drainage ditches

Introduction

The function of surface water drainage channels is to remove excess water so that farmland might be accessible to stock or machinery. They are particularly prevalent on grazing marsh areas, which now frequently include arable farming, and most especially in the intensively farmed landscapes of the Fens (Marshall, Wade & Clare 1978). They represent an important refuge for wetland plants and animals, although their value for nature conservation has diminished in recent years as traditional methods of management have given way either to over-engineered channels or neglect, resulting in poorer water quality, especially when combined with fertilizer runoff and pesticide inputs. Their value under set-aside can be increased by incorporating berms (shallow shelves close to the water level) on which reedbed vegetation can develop. Such areas are very efficient at filtering fertilizers and other pollutants from runoff before it reaches running open water, and they provide habitats for a range of declining species.

If the ditch is substantial enough, or if the field borders a stream or river, there may be opportunities to combine water margin management with trees, hedgerows and even wooded strips. Such diverse field margins will be valuable in areas for wildlife such as otters, as well as allowing the development of riverside walks and educational nature reserves.

Criteria for site selection

Selected sites will mostly be in the coastal levels and floodplains of major rivers, especially in the old grazing marshes of lowland England and Wales. There should be evidence of a rich aquatic macrophyte flora in the past (Mountford & Sheail 1989).

Information necessary to identify and define suitable sites

Target habitat Species-rich aquatic and marginal vegetation.

Location of site Particularly on flat land at low altitudes where surface water drainage is difficult.

Location of site in relation to target habitat distribution	Restoration is most important in the coastal levels where traditional grazing marsh has been largely converted to arable land (eg the Fenland and Romney Marsh). Successful restoration is most likely within the more extensive surviving grazing marshes of Somerset and Broadland. Propagules of macrophytes remain in the detritus at the bottom of existing channels, and a relaxation of more intensive management methods may allow a rich aquatic flora to develop.

Information necessary to assess the suitability of the site for restoration to the target habitat type

Most set-aside land will be inappropriate for restoring to aquatic macrophyte vegetation, because soils or topography are unsuitable. In some regions, however, existing channels may be managed for macrophytes or new channels created specifically for conservation.

Size	Existing drainage channels of all sizes are suitable, but any habitat creation should focus on the field ditch (c 1.5–2.5 m wide), which may be excavated readily. A shallow shelf below the water table (a berm) can be constructed on one side of the ditch extending into the set-aside land as required.
Soils	Restoration will be most successful on groundwater gley and peat soils, though surface water gleys and brown soils may also present opportunities. Natural macrophyte vegetation varies with the soil type. Soil fertility should be low to moderate, to reduce the spread of algae and aggressive species of eutrophic water, eg *Potamogeton pectinatus*.
Recent management history	Aquatic vegetation establishes quickly and many species are invasive. The composition

of the ditch vegetation depends on management and water quality. Provided management and nutrient inputs can be regulated during the set-aside phase, past management may be less important. However, sites which have received large fertilizer inputs, been managed with herbicides, or over-deepened are less likely to develop a rich aquatic flora.

Management on adjacent land
Establishment will be most successful where the neighbouring land is undrained and does not receive high inputs of fertilizer (although fertilizer inputs can be filtered to some extent by the grassland strip between the ditch and the cropped area). These criteria may also apply to land higher up the catchment, whose water drains through the set-aside ditch.

Proximity to existing habitat
Where set-aside is applied to an existing channel or to a newly dug ditch, success is most likely where the site is within the same watercourse network as ditches with a rich macrophyte vegetation. If such habitat is not adjacent, the influence of the nearby land may be deleterious and temporary isolation of the channel may need to be considered.

Checklist of additional features
Consider the position and function of the existing channel in the drainage network. Will managing the ditch under set-aside adversely affect the water regime of adjacent productive farmland?

Other designations/schemes
The management of grazing marsh ditches is an important part of all Tiers in some Environmentally Sensitive Areas (ESA), eg the Broads and Somerset Levels and Moors. Such areas may also be appropriate for the Countryside Stewardship Scheme (meadows and pastures).

Management

The management of drainage channels for nature conservation has been studied in considerable detail and there are numerous options for habitat creation (Newbold, Honnor & Buckley 1989). The important point is that wildlife will benefit from very simple measures, such as not using herbicides and instigating a two- or more year rotational management scheme so that ditches are not kept virtually free from vegetation. Ideally, ditch levels should be penned high to ensure that open water habitat is protected. Other prescriptions may be suggested, as follows.

- Where nature conservation is the main goal, consider dredging the ditch on a five-year rotational management, using a Bradshaw bucket, etc, or, where possible, manual techniques. The spoil should be heaped on one side of the watercourse only, leaving the vegetation intact on the other side.

- Where the agricultural production of the surrounding land remains the main consideration, but there is spare drainage capacity, treat the two sides of the channel differently. One bank and the adjacent water may be cut annually or more frequently, whilst the other may be cut on a longer rotational basis.

- Where the agricultural production of the surrounding land is paramount and there is no spare drainage capacity, but the farmer is prepared to sacrifice some productive land, a berm may be constructed in a widened ditch. This option may be the most appropriate for set-aside schemes; the rules allow a strip to be left uncut at the field boundary, 2 m wide, more if an exemption is granted.

Aim of management

To establish and maintain a variety of aquatic habitats within each watercourse, eg wet turf, shallow water and permanent deep water.

Site preparation techniques (if any)

If reedbeds are to be established, it should remembered that they should not be allowed to dry out, but should not become flooded to greater than 80 cm. Reeds can be planted from rhizomes or growing shoots in the spring (Osborne 1989).

Options for follow-up management

Reedbeds may require scrub clearance after 20 years or so.

Financial implications (capital and recurrent costs)

The use of manual methods or frequent (but restrained) use of machines and the excavation of new ditches or berms will incur costs. There may be implications for the water management of the whole catchment, requiring an integrated approach, and leading to off-site expenditure.

Potential off-site implications of different options

There may be possible impacts on the drainage of water from higher up the catchment, unless the drainage capacity is maintained with a berm. The berm (with, for example, a reedbed) and the macrophytes within the main channel may reduce the levels of nutrients in the drainage water downstream. Penned water levels may influence the productivity of adjacent land not within the set-aside scheme. Ditches bordered by unmanaged perennial vegetation including flowers such as great hairy willow-herb (*Epilobium hirsutum*) will support bumblebees, which can in turn pollinate nearby crops (Fussell & Corbett 1991, 1992).

The National Rivers Authority, regional drainage boards and local landowners may need to be consulted over changes in ditch management. Reedbeds can be placed to filter out fertilizer runoff at points of inflow.

Procedures and problems encountered for return to arable land

Replace any newly dug ditch with a piped drain.

Additional on-site implications of management

The drainage channel habitat is very valuable for birds, amphibians and particularly invertebrates. Waterfowlers and anglers may consider the increased aquatic habitat an advantage.

Timescales

Extensive macrophyte vegetation may establish in one season, although its composition will depend greatly on the propagules present. New species may easily be introduced using whole plants or fragments.

Potentially damaging operations

Such operations include the application and dumping of fertilizer and herbicide at any time, other than the spot treatment of weeds; excessive disturbance, should the site be used by waterfowl; and excessive pumping down of the water level. Dyke vegetation should not be burned.

Appraisal

The ditch should have a diverse macrophyte cover in the first season. Vegetation dominated by algae and water weeds (eg *Enteromorpha* spp., *Elodea nuttallii* or *Potamogeton pectinatus*) to the exclusion of most other species is unsuitable, and indicative that the water is too nutrient-rich.

Potential off-site impacts

Reduced nitrate runoff, but increased drainage problems for neighbouring land.

Implications for access

None. Paths could be created.

Woodland edge and hedgerow

Introduction

Hedges and woodlands are among our most characteristic landscape features, and have cultural and historical significance as well as value for wildlife (Pollard, Hooper & Moore 1974; Rackham 1986). Hedges are very important for many woodland margin and arable species. In general, the older the hedge, the greater its species richness, and some hedges have particular value as they are relics of ancient woodland, and still retain some of the ancient communities (Pollard 1973). The replacement of grazing by arable farming, and of horses by tractors, led to substantial removal of hedgerows, especially in the south and east of England. This removal continues today, and there is evidence that the many remaining hedges are suffering from neglect (Barr *et al.* 1991).

Hedges provide habitat for many species of plants, birds, mammals and insects, are thought to act as corridors for the dispersal of both woodland and arable species, and can act as sources for new areas of woodland and scrub on ungrazed set-aside arable land.

Taller, thicker hedges, especially if surrounded by meadow, support more bird species than short, frequently trimmed or gappy hedges. Ideally, there should be regular mature trees, and a high local density of hedgerow with plenty of intersections. Layering, coppicing or trimming should be carried out on a rotation around the farm of at least three years. The vegetation under and near the hedge is important for many species; an area of stinging nettle (*Urtica dioica*) supports many species of insects, including some of our best-known butterflies, such as the small tortoiseshell (*Aglais urticae*) and peacock (*Inachis io*).

Newly laid hedges should be planted with a diversity of species from the beginning; species numbers will increase with time, and according to distance from suitable sources of seed (other hedges and woodland).

One important option is to take advantage of the provision in the set-aside rules not to cut a 2 m strip of land next to the hedge, allowing the hedge to expand into a band of scrub along the edge of the field. This would be most successful where the hedge is already diverse, and has a high proportion of suckering (eg blackthorn (*Prunus spinosa*) and elm (*Ulmus* spp.)) and rambling (eg roses (*Rosa* spp.), brambles (*Rubus fruticosus*), etc) species which can encroach vegetatively into the new area. Scrub and woodland regeneration may be particularly valuable in upland areas where scrub regeneration has been reduced by grazing and land use changes (Peterken 1981; Good, Bryant & Carlill 1990).

Criteria for site selection

Information necessary to identify and define suitable sites

Target habitat	Hedgerow and/or scrub and adjacent ground flora.
Location of site	Not applicable, although hedges should not be encouraged in areas where field boundaries traditionally take the form of stone walls.
Location of site in relation to target habitat distribution	Not applicable, except for the extension of existing woodland, scrub or hedge into the field.

Information necessary to assess the suitability of the site for restoration to the target habitat type

Size	Any.
Soils	Not applicable.
Recent management history	Not applicable.
Management on adjacent land	The hedge and hedge bottom should not be subjected to drift of pesticides and

herbicides, but as there will be a grass buffer between the hedge and the cultivated part of the field, this should not be a problem.

Proximity to existing habitat   New hedges will increase in species richness more quickly if they are close to existing species-rich hedges or woodland.

Checklist of additional features
None.

Other designations/schemes
The Hedgerow Incentive Scheme and Environmentally Sensitive Areas are closely compatible with this option.

Management

There are three broad categories of management:

- to plant new hedges;
- to manage existing ones;
- to allow development of scrub from existing hedges and woodland.

For the wooded margins option of the Countryside Premium Scheme (Countryside Commission 1991), farmers were advised to establish a grass strip under the same rules as the grass margin (see below), and then to plant at least three of the following species to produce a hedge or wooded strip.

Oak	*Quercus robur*
Ash	*Fraxinus excelsior*
Hawthorn	*Crataegus laevigata/monogyna*
Blackthorn	*Prunus spinosa*
Crab apple	*Malus sylvestris*
Field maple	*Acer campestre*
Hazel	*Corylus avellana*
Dogwood	*Cornus sanguinea*
Buckthorn	*Rhamnus catharticus*
Spindle	*Euonymus europaeus*
Wild cherry	*Prunus avium*
Guelder rose	*Viburnum opulus*
Holly	*Ilex aquifolia*
Dog rose	*Rosa canina*

The following species were also allowed if a woodland strip was desired.

Aspen	*Populus tremula*
Sallow	*Salix caprea*
Crack willow	*Salix fragilis*
Alder	*Alnus glutinosa*
Silver birch	*Betula pendula*
Downy birch	*Betula pubescens*

The choice of species can be guided by those found in nearby hedges, and depends on soil type.

Existing hedges should be made continuous, if not already, by planting gaps with species from the above lists and by layering. In some cases, such as along some roadsides, the hedge may need to be kept low for safety; otherwise, the objective should be to establish a rotation of hedge management on the farm, allowing the development of hedges at least 2 m tall and 1 m wide. As the timing of management and shape of the hedge subtly alter the wildlife complement (eg partridges (*Perdix perdix*) prefer low, narrow hedges with grassy, hedge bottom vegetation), the shape of the hedge should be varied within the farm, or accord with local tradition. Management can consist of trimming (not more than once every three years, and preferably at the end of the winter, after seeds and berries have been eaten but before nesting), laying (not more than once every eight years) and coppicing (not more than once every 15 years) (Deane 1989). In many landscapes, it is worth identifying saplings which will be allowed to become emergent trees, as this will increase the use of the hedge by birds (Lack 1992).

The hedge bottom flora may be similar to grassland, or composed largely of arable grass weeds, in which case it should be replaced, if necessary, and managed as meadow strip (see below). It may include elements of woodland flora, including bluebells (*Hyacinthoides non-scripta*) and dog's mercury (*Mercurialis perennis*), which would benefit from a long rotation between hedge mowing and laying treatments. Hedges and scrub containing brambles with hedge bottom flora including labiates such as black horehound (*Ballota nigra*) and white dead-nettle (*Lamium album*) will benefit bumblebees which can in turn pollinate crops such as rape and field beans (Fussell & Corbet 1991). Bumblebee areas should be relatively undisturbed, and should provide a sequence of pollen sources (see Fussell & Corbet 1992 for details).

Expansion of hedgerows into scrub and woodland strips can be achieved by allowing natural regeneration, especially if the hedge is already diverse and includes species able to spread vegetatively, or by planting the species in the above lists (or, better, by using cuttings from any of the species present in the hedge itself) in the desired area. Planting can be used to create a second hedge, creating a lane for public access on the set-aside land.

Aim of management
To plant new hedges, and/or to manage existing hedges, and/or to allow scrub development from a hedge.

Site preparation techniques (if any)
Not applicable.

Options for follow-up management
The hedge can be maintained, or allowed to expand. Grazing must be prevented during the establishment phase, which could be as long as ten years in some upland areas.

Financial implications (capital and recurrent costs)
Hedge establishment involves capital costs, and maintenance is also required; rough costings are provided by Deane (1989). There may be a need to maintain fences to prevent accidental grazing events in some instances.

Potential off-site implications of different options
Not applicable.

Procedures and problems encountered for return to arable land
In all cases, return to arable land will be expensive, requiring grubbing out the wooded species and preparing the soil anew. This option should not be adopted if an early return to arable land is envisaged.

Additional on-site implications for management

The quality and nature of the flora and fauna will vary greatly, but it is possible that pest species such as rabbits (*Oryctolagus cuniculus*) will be encouraged.

Timescales

The timescale for scrub encroachment is in the region of ten years for the suckering and spreading species noted above, longer for others (Deane 1989).

Potentially damaging operations

In general, herbicides should not be applied; if the hedge bottom contains high proportions of potential weeds such as barren brome (*Bromus sterilis*) or couch-grass (*Elymus repens*), it should be managed as a meadow strip (see below); a case can sometimes be made for applying suitable specific herbicides (see Game Conservancy 1992). Attempts to control these species using broad-spectrum herbicides alone are unlikely to prove effective in the long term (Smith & Macdonald 1992).

Appraisal

A greater diversity of plants and animals should be recorded. Hedgerow birds may be slow in colonising new plantings, but would be expected to appear within five years.

Potential off-site impacts

The hedge may well shade land on neighbouring fields. It will also act as a reservoir for beneficial (eg bumblebees, predatory insects), attractive (eg butterflies) and pest (eg rabbits and, in larger scrub areas, foxes (*Vulpes vulpes*)) species.

Implications for access

The hedgerow can be combined with grass access paths, which would be particularly appreciated in areas currently dominated by intensive arable agriculture. Styles and gates may be needed. Such areas may qualify for the Countryside Access Scheme.

Meadow strip

Introduction

A meadow strip will be required between the field boundary
vegetation and the cropped area. In conventional field borders, this
is very narrow or absent altogether, but in set-aside field margins its
width should be highly variable. It is used to provide a diversity of
habitat, a buffer between the cropped area and the field boundary
vegetation, public access, and access and turning space for
machinery. The strip itself should be managed as a mosaic of short
and longer grasses. Many species will benefit, notably the barn owl
(*Tyto alba*), provided that nearby nesting sites are available (Lack
1992). The management of this strip is the same as for meadow;
there is a choice between managing natural regeneration in the
case of sites with few weed problems and suitable flora in the seed
bank or in the existing field margin, and sowing suitable seed
mixtures. This section will concentrate on the use of sown grass
covers; see Chapter 8 for further details of managing natural
regeneration.

Criteria for site selection

Information necessary to identify and define suitable sites

Target habitat	Species-rich meadow, dominated by perennial grasses and forbs.
Location of site	Not applicable.
Location of site in relation to target habitat distribution	Not applicable.

Information necessary to assess the suitability of the site for restoration to the target habitat type
Management history and weed infestation should be considered by
the farmer.

Size	Any.

Soils	Clay soils tend to be dominated by pernicious weeds. If so, sown cover will be preferrable to natural regeneration, which can easily give rise to dense swards of couch-grass and similar problem species.

Recent management history	A field margin with a long history of intensive management (ie high nutrient level, high pesticide levels, weeds mostly grass) is probably best put under sown cover. Otherwise, natural regeneration should be allowed.

Management on adjacent land	Natural regeneration will be more effective if neighbouring margins and land have populations of grassland species, perennial and biennial flowers.

Proximity to existing adjacent land	See above.

Checklist of additional features
None.

Other designations/schemes
May be compatible with Nitrate Sensitive Areas.

Management

Management can be either natural regeneration or sown grassland cover, the decision depending largely on the potential for regenerating a forb-rich sward on the one hand, or high densities of grass weeds on the other. The management of natural regeneration is described below (Chapter 8); there should be a mosaic of areas cut once a year and areas cut more than once.

The sown cover would entail sowing a grassland mixture. The land may need to be treated with a herbicide such as glyphosate before sowing to reduce levels of perennial weeds (Deane 1989).

Three kinds of grass mixture should be considered for three kinds of management:

- fine, low grass, to support wild flowers, associated insects and insectivorous birds;
- tall, coarser vegetation for small mammals, some birds and bumblebees; and
- a more robust, short turf in areas subjected to frequent trampling or compaction.

The Countryside Premium Scheme meadowland option required the sowing of native grasses particularly suited to fine grassy swards:

Common bent-grass	*Agrostis capillaris*
Meadow foxtail	*Alopecurus pratensis*
Sweet vernal-grass	*Anthoxanthum odoratum*
Crested dog's-tail	*Cynosurus cristatus*
Sheep's fescue	*Festuca ovina*
Meadow fescue	*Festuca pratensis*
Red fescue	*Festuca rubra commutata*
Smooth-stalked meadow-grass	*Poa pratensis*
Yellow oat	*Trisetum flavescens*
Small-leaved timothy	*Phleum pratense bertolonii*

The Countryside Commission required that the sward should be cut at least three times between 1 May and 31 October in the first year (Countryside Commission 1991), but twice may be enough (H Smith, pers. comm.). Thereafter, parts of the field should be allowed to grow long, by cutting once between 1 September and 31 March (ensuring that some long grass is left over winter), and the rest of the field should be kept short by mowing or cutting regularly during the spring and summer to keep the grass no higher than 15 cm. Cuttings must be left on the ground to rot, but mounds of cuttings may provide overwintering areas for reptiles, and support a range of fungi and insects (Deane 1989) (NB making sure that any flora of interest are not buried). Light grazing is permitted between 1 September and 14 January (as long as the cover is cut between 15 July and 15 August), but is unlikely to be practical on many field margins.

The value of the grass sward to wildlife can be enhanced by including wildflower seeds. These can be expensive, they may not represent genotypes well suited to local conditions, and not all species in a typical mixture will establish (Deane 1989; Wells, Cox & Frost 1989a,b). One should, therefore, select species known to be common locally, eg by sowing seeds of one or two species found in nearby hedgerows, or by the less reliable technique of sowing seeds harvested from nearby hay meadows to preserve local genetic variability (Wells, Frost & Bell 1986). Typical example species for a fine sward may be:

Yarrow	*Achillea millefolium*
Ox-eye daisy	*Leucanthemum vulgare*
Ribwort	*Plantago lanceolata*
Cowslip	*Primula veris*
Self-heal	*Prunella vulgaris*
Meadow buttercup	*Ranunculus acris*
Common sorrel	*Rumex acetosa*
Salad burnet	*Sanguisorba minor*
Musk mallow	*Malva moschata*
White campion	*Silene alba*
Black medick	*Medicago lupulina*
Lesser knapweed	*Centauria nigra*

For a coarser, taller sward, species could include (Deane 1989):

Oat-grass	*Arrhenatherum elatius*
Cock's-foot	*Dactylis glomerata*
Tall fescue	*Festuca arundinacea*
Yorkshire fog	*Holcus lanatus*
Tufted hair-grass (for wetter soils)	*Deschampsia cespitosa*
Teasel	*Dipsacus fullonum*
Wild carrot	*Daucus carota*
Upright hedge-parsley	*Torilis japonica.*

Ideally, there should be an unbroken sequence of nectar sources for butterflies and other nectar feeders; ox-eye daisy and greater (*Centaurea scabiosa)* or lesser knapweed is a good combination for butterflies (H Smith, pers. comm.). Areas likely to be used frequently for access may need to have harder-wearing grasses, such as perennial rye-grass (*Lolium perenne*), included in the seed mixture – these grasses should be avoided elsewhere (Deane 1989).

In all cases, seed rates are variable. Reduced rates are cheaper, allow more space for natural invasion from other species, but are susceptible to invasion by unwanted weed species, require frequent mowing for longer periods, and take longer to achieve a complete sward. Deane (1989) suggests 10–20 kg ha^{-1}; a field margin management experiment at Oxford used 30 kg ha^{-1} (H Smith, pers. comm.). Another possibility is to use a nurse crop of annual rye-grass, and then prevent it seeding by cutting (Wells, Cox & Frost 1989a,b). However, this is expensive, and the nurse may be too vigorous in fertile soils (Deane 1989).

The use of flail mowing reduces problems arising from leaving cuttings (Deane 1989). If coarse grass stands become too uniform, a two-cut regime (May and August) can be introduced in some areas to increase plant diversity (Parr & Way 1988). If cutting is required before mid-July, farmers should try to reduce damage to wildlife by discouraging nesting birds, by beginning mowing early in the year, by cutting to the maximum safe height, and by mowing in directions allowing wildlife the chance to escape.

Aim of management
To produce a flower-rich grass sward with a mixture of tall and short stands.

Site preparation techniques (if any)
It may be necessary to reduce the burden of perennial weeds such as couch-grass. This can be achieved by applying glyphosate before sowing in the autumn. In extreme cases, a seed bed should be prepared in the autumn, and sprayed with glyphosate in the spring before the grass is sown (Deane 1989). If the land to be set-aside is already grassland, its wildflower diversity can be enhanced by slot seeding (Wells, Cox & Frost 1989a,b).

Options for follow-up management
Grazing should be considered if practical. It creates gaps in the sward which can speed up colonisation of new plant species, while dung and urine create new microhabitats and tend to increase botanical diversity (Deane 1989; Treweek 1990), but at the expense of

some insect groups (Treweek 1990), notably cranefly larvae (*Tipula* spp.) (Bignal & McCracken 1993) which are important food for skylarks (*Alauda arvensis*) and gamebirds.

Financial implications (capital and recurrent costs)

The establishment of sown cover incurs seed costs, which can be reduced by adopting shorter species lists. The choice of cutting regime incurs small annual costs.

Potential off-site implications of different options

There are risks of weed seed, pest and disease spread to the main and adjacent fields. The risks of disease spread are probably small (Yarham & Symonds 1992), and ingress of seeds will be slight if the cover is kept short near the main field. The barley yellow dwarf virus-transmitting aphids *Sitobion avenae* and *Rhopalosiphum padi* overwinter on grass (Hand 1989; Carter & Plumb 1991).

If the coarse grass mixture is grown adjacent to the cropped areas, increases should be observed in the populations of insect predators, such as carabid beetles, which will then move into the crop (Thomas, Wratten & Sotherton 1992; Kielty, Allen-Williams & Underwood 1992). Spear thistle (*Cirsium vulgare*), autumnal hawkbit (*Leontodon autumnalis*) and white campion can be sown at the margin of the cropped area to provide food for hoverflies, whose larvae are valuable predators of aphids in crops (Wratten & Powell 1991).

Procedures and problems encountered for return to arable land

Potential weed problems can be anticipated by using sown covers on fields heavily infested with grass weeds, and alleviated after set-aside by using a break crop such as beans, allowing the effective use of grass weed herbicides.

Additional on-site implications for management

Sown covers can give good control of agricultural weeds after one year (Smith & Macdonald 1989, 1992).

Timescales

For details of natural regeneration, see Chapter 8. If the cover is

sown, birds and insects should benefit in the second year. Its value
will increase as more species of plants and insects colonise naturally.

Potentially damaging operations

These include the application and drift of fertilizer or herbicides
(except where indicated), and mowing between March and 10
August, except in the first year of sown cover, and in short grass
areas.

Appraisal

Appraisal for sown grass cover will include the establishment of sown
species (including flowers), and a reduction in the extent of bare soil
after two years. Appraisal for natural regeneration is as Chapter 8.

Potential off-site impacts

There will be substantial improvement in quality of runoff water; field
margins will also act as buffer areas against spray drift.

Implications for access

Long grass areas should not be greatly disturbed during April–July,
but casual walkers would be quite acceptable, especially along
designated paths.

References

Barr, C.J., Howard, D.C., Bunce, R.G.H., Gillespie, M.K. & Hallam, C.J. 1991.
Changes in hedgerows in Britain between 1984 and 1990. (NERC contract report to
the Department of the Environment.) Grange-over-Sands: Institute of Terrestrial
Ecology.

Bignal, E. & McCracken, D. 1993. Nature conservation and pastoral farming in the
British uplands. *British Wildlife,* **4**, 367–376.

Bunce, R.G.H. & Howard, D.C. 1990. *Species dispersal in agricultural habitats.*
London: Belhaven.

Carter, N. & Plumb, R.T. 1991. The epidemiology of cereal viruses. In: *The ecology of temperate cereal fields*, edited by L.G. Firbank, N. Carter, J.F. Darbyshire & G.R. Potts, 193–208. Oxford: Blackwell Scientific.

Countryside Commission. 1991. *The countryside premium for set-aside land.* Cambridge: Countryside Commission.

Deane, R.J.L. 1989. *Expanded field margins. Their costs to the farmer and benefits to wildlife.* (Report to the Nature Conservancy Council.) Tewkesbury: Kemerton Court.

Fussell, M. & Corbet, S.A. 1991. Forage for bumble bees and honey bees in farmland: a case study. *Journal of Apicultural Research,* **30,** 87–97.

Fussell, M. & Corbet, S.A. 1992. Flower use by bumble-bees: a basis for forage plant management. *Journal of Applied Ecology,* **29,** 451–465.

Game Conservancy. 1992. *Guidelines 1992/93: management of Conservation Headlands.* Fordingbridge: Game Conservancy.

Good, J.E.G., Bryant, R. & Carlill, P. 1990. Distribution, longevity and survival of upland hawthorn (*Crataegus monogyna*) scrub in north Wales in relation to sheep grazing. *Journal of Applied Ecology,* **27,** 272–283.

Hand, S.C. 1989. The overwintering of cereal aphids on Graminae in southern England, 1977–1980. *Annals of Applied Biology,* **115,** 17–29.

Kielty, J.P., Allen-Williams, L.J. & Underwood, N. 1992. The effects of set-aside field margins on the distribution and biocontrol potential of polyphagous predatory arthropods in arable crops. In: *Set-aside,* edited by J. Clarke, 169–174. Farnham: British Crop Protection Council.

Lack, P. 1992. *Birds on lowland farms.* London: HMSO.

Marshall, E.J.P., Wade, P.M. & Clare, P. 1978. Land drainage channels in England and Wales. *Geographical Journal,* **144,** 254–263.

Mountford, J.O. & Sheail, J. 1989. *The effects of agricultural land use change on the flora of three grazing marsh areas.* (Focus on nature conservation no. 20.) Peterborough: Nature Conservancy Council.

Newbold, C., Honnor, J. & Buckley, K. 1989. *Nature conservation and the management of drainage channels.* Peterborough: Nature Conservancy Council.

Osborne, P. 1989. *The management of set-aside land for birds: a practical guide.* Sandy: Royal Society for the Protection of Birds.

Parr, T.W. & Way, J.M. 1988. Management of roadside vegetation: the long-term effects of cutting. *Journal of Applied Ecology,* **25,** 1073–1087.

Peterken, G.F. 1981. *Woodland conservation and management.* London: Chapman & Hall.

Pollard, E. 1973. Hedges. VII. Woodland relic hedges in Huntingdon and Peterborough. *Journal of Ecology,* **61**, 343–352.

Pollard, E., Hooper, M.D. & Moore, N.W. 1974. *Hedges.* London: Collins.

Rackham, O. 1986. *The history of the countryside.* London: Dent.

Smith, H. & Macdonald, D.W. 1989. Secondary succession on extended arable field margins: its manipulation for wildlife benefit and weed control. In: *Brighton Crop Protection Conference – Weeds 1989,* 1063–1068. Farnham: British Crop Protection Council.

Smith, H. & Macdonald, D.W. 1992. The impacts of mowing and sowing on weed populations and species richness in field margin set-aside. In: *Set-aside,* edited by J. Clarke, 117–122. Farnham: British Crop Protection Council.

Sotherton, N.W., Boatman, N.D. & Robertson, P.A. 1992. The use of set-aside land for game conservation. In: *Set-aside,* edited by J. Clarke, 223–228. Farnham: British Crop Protection Council.

Thomas, M.B., Wratten, S.D. & Sotherton, N.W. 1991. Creation of 'island' habitats in farmland to manipulate populations of beneficial arthropods: predator densities and emigration. *Journal of Applied Ecology,* **28**, 906–917.

Treweek, J.R. 1990. *The ecology of sheep grazing: its use in nature conservation management of lowland neutral grassland.* DPhil thesis, University of Oxford.

Wells, T.C.E., Cox, R. & Frost, A. 1989a. Diversifying grasslands by introducing seed and transplants into existing vegetation. In: *Biological habitat reconstruction,* edited by G.P. Buckley, 283–298. London: Belhaven.

Wells, T.C.E., Cox, R. & Frost, A. 1989b. *The establishment and management of wild flower meadows.* Peterborough: Nature Conservancy Council.

Wells, T.C.E., Frost, A. & Bell, S.A. 1986. *Wild flower grasslands from crop-grown seed and hay-bales.* (Focus on nature conservation no.15.) Peterborough: Nature Conservancy Council.

Wratten, S.D. & Powell, W. 1991. Cereal aphids and their natural enemies. In: *The ecology of temperate cereal fields,* edited by L.G. Firbank, N. Carter, J.F. Darbyshire & G.R. Potts, 233–257. Oxford: Blackwell Scientific.

Yarham, D.J. & Symonds, B.V. 1992. Effects of set-aside on diseases of cereals. In: *Set-aside,* edited by J. Clarke, 41–46. Farnham: British Crop Protection Council.

7 SET-ASIDE FOR OTTER HAVENS

Summary

Otters and other wildlife will benefit from setting aside riverside areas where disturbance and pollution are minimised, and where there is vegetation cover in the form of scrub and wooded areas.

Introduction

The otter (*Lutra lutra*) is our only EC Habitats Directive terrestrial mammal (Commission of the European Communities 1992), and is scarce throughout much of its range. It is always found near water, and seldom tolerates the presence of people. Its numbers have declined as a result of habitat loss, disturbance, road traffic and pollution, but there are now signs of recovery, especially in south-west England and Wales (Strachan *et al.* 1990). Set-aside provides an opportunity to increase the number of otter havens, while simultaneously providing habitat for waterside birds, plants and insects. No-one can guarantee the use by otters of any particular haven, but a network of these sites will certainly bring benefit to the species as a whole. Otter havens are permitted under non-rotational set-aside, provided an exemption is sought from the cutting regulations. In cases where substantial vegetation regrowth is needed, havens are best regarded as a longer-term option, suitable for entry under the Habitat Scheme as either water fringe habitats (in pilot areas only) or, where appropriate, as valuable habitats created under the five-year set-aside scheme.

Many of these recommendations are taken from King and Potter (undated).

Criteria for site selection

Information necessary to identify and define suitable sites

Target habitat   Undisturbed river banks with well-developed vegetation.

Location of site	Otters are found across Britain, notably in Scotland, Wales and the north and south-west of England (Strachan *et al.* 1990). However, otters range widely, and it is wise not to rely simply on survey records. Therefore, while the river should ideally be known to support otters already, this is not essential. Otter havens may be of particular value in areas of East Anglia where otters have been released into the wild (Strachan *et al.* 1990).
	The haven may be on the main river or along a tributary or side stream.
Location of site in relation to target habitat distribution	Otter territories can extend as long as 40 km, and there must be secure holts and staging posts at intervals. Therefore, new havens should be along the same river systems, and within 1 km of currently suitable or newly created habitat.

Information necessary to assess the suitability of the site for restoration to the target habitat type

The water must contain plenty of fish, and the river must suffer little disturbance. Ideally, riverside vegetation should already comprise mature waterside trees, especially oak (*Quercus* spp.), ash (*Fraxinus excelsior*) and sycamore (*Acer pseudoplatanus*).

Size	The new haven should be at least 400 m long, and extend at least 200 m from the bank.
Soils	Not applicable.
Recent management history	Ideally, large waterside trees should already exist.
Management on adjacent land	The key points are lack of disturbance and lack of pollution. Set-aside or grazed low-input grasslands and woodlands would be appropriate adjacent land uses.

Proximity to existing   Within 1 km.
habitat

Checklist of additional features
There should be a history of otters along the river system. Suitable indicator species include kingfisher (*Alcedo atthis*).

Other designations/schemes
This prescription is compatible with Environmentally Sensitive and Nitrate Sensitive Area schemes, and the waterside landscape option of the Countryside Stewardship Scheme.

Management

In general, natural regeneration should be allowed along one or ideally both sides of the river. However, if the amount of cover is currently very small, then it will be desirable to plant trees and shrubs (Chapter 6, adding evergreen bushes such as holly (*Ilex aquifolium*)), and to encourage water fringe vegetation (Chapter 6). Clumps of trees are better than riverside lines of trees. The area further than 50 m away from the water's edge should be managed as set-aside natural regeneration or sown cover (Chapter 8).

Another alternative is to create cover over a ditch or side stream to connect the river with an existing woodland or dense scrub area.

Aim of management
To allow the development of dense waterside vegetation, and the creation of a buffer zone between it and arable farming operations.

Site preparation techniques (if any)
See Chapters 6 and 8 if appropriate.

Options for follow-up management
Pollarding and/or coppicing could be practised. Occasional drag-lining may be required.

Financial implications (capital and recurrent costs)
There should be few recurrent costs except those associated with any coppicing, pollarding and the removal of trees which become dangerous for some reason; there may be capital costs associated with tree planting.

Potential off-site implications of different options
The main off-site implication is for the use of the river by pleasure boats and walkers – the less disturbance, the better.

Procedures and problems encountered for return to arable land
This option is not easily compatible for a return to arable land.

Additional on-site implications of management
Other species will benefit, notably kingfisher and sand martin (*Riparia riparia*) if there are steep sandy banks for nesting in open areas.

Timescales
The timescale depends on the maturity of the vegetation; some areas will bring benefits within a year, by removing farming operations from areas close to habitats which are otherwise already suitable. Restoration from an arable field directly bordering a river could take between five and 15 years before it becomes suitable for otters.

Potentially damaging operations
Holts should not be disturbed; power tools especially must not be used.

Appraisal
Success is proven only by evidence of otters using the site. However, it may be reasonable to use evidence of otters using the river system within a certain distance of the site, or to use some other index of suitability, eg the presence of kingfishers.

Potential off-site impacts
There may be improvements in water quality. There may be increases in numbers of foxes (*Vulpes vulpes*) and rabbits (*Oryctolagus cuniculus*).

Implications for access

All access is harmful, whether by vehicles to the vicinity, walkers or access by boat along the river, but very low levels of disturbance will be tolerated if the otters can easily escape via undergrowth. Otter set-aside should not be used for angling.

References

Commission of the European Communities. 1992. Council Directive 92/43/EEC of 21 May 1992 on the conservation of natural habitats and of wild fauna and flora. *Official Journal of the European Communities*, L 206, 7–50.

King, A. & Potter, A. Undated. *A guide to otter conservation for water authorities.* London: Vincent Wildlife Trust.

Strachan, R., Birks, J.D.S., Chanin, P.F.R. & Jefferies, D.J. 1990. *Otter survey of England 1984–1986.* Peterborough: Nature Conservancy Council.

8 NATURAL REGENERATION AND SOWN COVER

Summary

Non-rotational set-aside can be used to create a wide diversity within fields, within regions and between years by combining management regimes. Different cutting regimes applied to a naturally regenerating field can be particularly valuable where pernicious weed problems are not too great.

Introduction

Naturally regenerating set-aside land undergoes a succession from dominance by volunteer cereals and annual weeds to perennial grasses and forbs, and, given time and left alone, will usually revert to scrub and woodland. The rate of change depends upon local factors, notably the seed bank and the proximity of potential colonising plant species. Thus, an area recently ploughed from permanent pasture will develop a pasture-like community much faster than an area which has long been under intensive agriculture, where the main early colonists would be weeds and volunteers. Likewise, invasion by scrub and woodland is most likely to take place by encroachment and dispersal from a hedge or wood adjoining the field. If marginal upland land is being set-aside, then natural regeneration is likely to be slower than in the lowlands.

Natural regeneration, therefore, does not restore particular habitats so much as promoting sequences of habitats. These sequences can be controlled to some extent by management (eg annual cutting will prevent the development of scrub), but also depend on local conditions.

Within these successional sequences are habitats which are important to many species. The winter stubble for the first year provides important seed sources to many of our wintering birds, and may provide opportunities for the increase of rare arable weeds. The increase of perennials can support the habitat structure and species of flowers which will boost populations of many species of bumblebees, butterflies and small mammals. A mown sward can provide habitats for the more prostrate plant species and their associated herbivores, while providing feeding areas for lapwings (*Vanellus vanellus*) and other birds. Scrub and early successional woodland meet the requirements of many of the species associated with hedgerow and woodland edge, notably birds such as warblers.

The most important endpoint of natural regeneration is, therefore, habitat diversity. This can be achieved within the field by managing different parts of the field differently; one may, for example, keep an area in the centre of the field as mixed-length grassland (which could revert to arable after a few years, if wished), and allow scrub invasion at parts of the field boundary. Such diversity gives benefits over and above those provided by the separate habitats; for example, the mixture of tall and short grasses is ideal for owls, as small mammals breed in the tall grasses but can be caught when traversing the short grass areas. Diversity can be managed on a larger scale by having non-rotational set-aside beginning at different times within the course of the set-aside scheme, or by having cycles of several years of set-aside and several years of cropping on particular fields.

The sowing of plant species provides a further alternative for non-rotational set-aside land. Sown covers can be used to introduce plants into set-aside land much quicker than would usually happen under natural regeneration, and can be used to tailor the area for particular species and species groups, such as butterflies, bumblebees and game birds.

Brent geese (*Branta bernicla bernicla*) feeding areas and stone curlew (*Burhinus oedicnemus*) habitats can also be created under non-rotational set-aside; these are dealt with separately in the following chapters.

Criteria for site selection

Information necessary to identify and define suitable sites

Target habitat	Precise objectives are variable; they will often be to allow a succession, rather than to create a habitat.
Location of site	Not applicable.
Location of site in relation to target habitat distribution	Not applicable.

Information necessary to assess the suitability of the site for restoration to the target habitat type

Management history and weed infestation should be considered by the farmer.

Size	Any.
Soils	Clay soils tend to be dominated by pernicious weeds. When these are present, sown cover will be preferable to natural regeneration, which can easily give rise to dense swards of couch-grass (*Elymus repens*) and similar problem species.
Recent management history	A field with a long history of intensive management (ie high nutrient level, high pesticide levels, weeds mostly grass) is probably best put under sown cover. Fields recently converted from a land use such as pasture or heathland should be considered for restoration. Otherwise, natural regeneration should be allowed.

Management on adjacent land	Not applicable.

Proximity to existing habitat	Natural regeneration will be more effective if neighbouring land (the field margins and slightly beyond) have populations of grassland species, perennial and biennial flowers, woodland and scrub plants, etc.

Checklist of additional features
None.

Other designations/schemes
Compatible with Environmentally Sensitive Areas, and some options for Nitrate Sensitive Areas.

Management

Natural regeneration
No management
No management will allow gradual conversion to perennial grassland, scrub and eventually woodland. However, successional stages could include thickets of brambles (*Rubus* spp.), nettles (*Urtica* spp.) and thistles (*Sonchus* spp.) – good for birds and insects, but untidy. Some paths and patches may need to be cut for access; see options below. Natural regeneration of broadleaved woodland and scrub adjacent to existing habitats in the uplands and upland margins would be a valuable, but long-term option, and accidental episodes of grazing would need to be prevented for several years. This option will require an exemption from the requirement to cut.

One cut each year
Cutting once each year will prevent succession to scrub and wood. The timing of the cut is important – the period of bird nesting and butterfly activity, from March to mid-September, should be avoided if possible. If the land is to be grazed during the late autumn, the cover must be cut between 15 July and 15 August – this operation should be carried out as late as possible.

More than one cut each year

This regime will keep the sward low, may increase plant diversity, and can help reduce the dominance of coarse grasses such as oat-grass (*Arrhenatherum elatius*) and couch-grass (Parr & Way 1988), although it may encourage the persistence of arable grass weeds (Smith & Macdonald 1992). Cuts should take place from the centre of the field outwards, and should avoid mid-March–May. Limited grazing in the autumn should also increase plant diversity.

Long-term cutting experiments have shown that the choice of machine appears to make little difference to the vegetation, whereas increasing the cutting frequency slightly increased sward diversity (Parr & Way 1988).

Annual minimum cultivation

This can be justified to maintain open conditions for rare arable weeds, ground-nesting birds and cirl bunting (*Emberiza cirlus*) on relatively infertile soils. The land should be lightly disced (to no more than 7 cm) in March and, if necessary, in September each year, and the vegetation cut once only between September and March each year (Osborne 1989). An exemption to the set-aside rules is needed. This is the same as the Countryside Premium Scheme wildlife fallow option (Countryside Commission 1991), which has been notable for very high populations of dragonflies, grasshoppers and butterflies (A Rutherford, pers. comm.).

For cirl bunting, the cultivated area should be rich in broadleaved weeds, and be close to untrimmed scrub or hedged where the birds nest. This species has a very local distribution, and special advice should be sought from the Royal Society for the Protection of Birds if it nests close to potential set-aside land.

A specialised version of this option aimed particularly at the stone curlew is described separately in Chapter 10.

Annual sown covers

Annual cover crop mixtures and annual tillage perpetuate the rotational set-aside for birds, and spring-sown cover crop mixtures (eg swedes and cereals) can be used to provide effective cover the following winter (Sotherton, Boatman & Robertson 1992).

All of the above options can be combined within a field to create a mosaic of habitats attractive to people and rich in wildlife.

Perennial sown covers
Details are the same as those given under the 'meadow strip' section (Chapter 6).

Aim of management
To allow succession to take place, or to arrest the system at a given successional stage, generating a diversity of habitats at a local level.

Site preparation techniques (if any)
None are required. However, the farmer may wish to exercise weed control in the first year; this control can be achieved by using either selective herbicides approved for use in Conservation Headlands (Game Conservancy 1992). Cutting in spring or early summer can also provide effective weed control if carefully timed (Smith & Macdonald 1992), but is damaging to nesting birds.

Options for follow-up management
Moderate levels of grazing encourage the development of a more diverse sward by creating gaps (Gibson & Brown 1991); this practice is allowed under the set-aside rules in the autumn, provided that the cover is cut between 15 July and 15 August. Native trees can be planted to provide a wood pasture or parkland habitat, which would greatly benefit woodland edge species, but does risk diluting local genetic populations.

Financial implications (capital and recurrent costs)
The establishment of sown cover incurs seed costs, although these can be minimised by reducing the number of species used. There will be small annual costs arising from cutting, and in some cases maintaining fences.

Potential off-site implications of different options
Sown cover will reduce the risk of build-up of weeds and of some diseases.

Procedures and problems encountered for return to arable land
The cover needs to be mown, and the land cultivated as appropriate. The likely build-up of annual plants in the first year or two generates a very large seed rain (Jones & Naylor 1992), but it is unclear how much penetrates into the seed bank – it is possible that many of the seeds are eaten by birds and small mammals. While Clarke and Cooper (1992) reported no seed problems in crops following set-aside (including sown cover and natural regeneration), all their plots had been cut at least once a year. Weed problems can be mitigated by using sown covers on fields heavily infested with grass weeds, and alleviated after set-aside by using a break crop such as beans, and allowing the effective use of grass weed herbicides. Diseases are likely to be suppressed by longer-term fallows (Fry 1982). Scrub can be removed by machinery.

Additional on-site implications for management
The management suggested here conflicts with the use of spring and summer cutting regimes to control grass weeds (Carter 1990; Smith & Macdonald 1992). Any rare arable weeds are likely to be lost after several years (sooner under sown covers), except under the annual minimum cultivation option.

Timescales
Precise timescales are variable depending upon local conditions. Under natural regeneration from long-established arable land, the first year is typified by substantial bare ground, volunteers and weeds. There follows ingress of species typical of disturbed habitats, such as ragworts and groundsels (*Senecio* spp.), willow-herbs (*Epilobium* spp.) and thistles, followed again by increases in perennials, and ultimately trees and shrubs (eg Wilson 1992). The initial appearance of these groups is not in a set sequence; for example, tree seedlings have been observed in the first year (Wilson 1992), but it is a while before these grow sufficiently to dominate the area.

The dynamics of the community also depend upon local grazing by domestic livestock, deer and rabbits, which can speed up the appearance of short-lived species (eg Gibson & Brown 1991), as well as prevent establishment of trees and shrubs.

Potentially damaging operations
Such operations include the application of fertilizer or herbicides (except spot or selective treatments where required), and mowing during the breeding season, except in the first year of sown cover, and in short grass areas.

Appraisal

Appraisal depends upon the type of management adopted. There should be increases in the numbers of birds, small mammals and common orders of insects on the set-aside land compared with adjacent arable land; there is scope for appraisal using plant species presence, diversity and plant structure.

Potential off-site impacts

The risks of disease spread to neighbouring fields are probably small (Yarham & Symonds 1992), and the migration of weed seeds from set-aside to neighbouring fields is almost entirely restricted to field margins (Jones & Naylor 1992). There may, however, be substantial increases in rabbits (Boag 1992). Nitrate leaching will decline with time.

Implications for access

Long grass areas should not be greatly disturbed during April–July, but a low level of casual walkers would be quite acceptable. Paths can be created under the Countryside Access Scheme.

References

Boag, B. 1992. Effect of set-aside on soil nematode fauna and vertebrates in eastern Scotland. In: *Set-aside*, edited by J. Clarke, 153–158. Farnham: British Crop Protection Council.

Carter, E.S. 1990. Weed control in amenity areas and other non-agricultrual land. In: *Weed control handbook: principles*, edited by R.J. Hance & K. Holly, 431–455. Oxford: Blackwell Scientific.

Clarke, J.H. & Cooper, F.B. 1992. Vegetation changes and weed levels in set-aside and subsequent crops. In: *Set-aside*, edited by J. Clarke, 103–110. Farnham: British Crop Protection Council.

Countryside Commission. 1991. *The countryside premium for set-aside land.* Cambridge: Countryside Commission.

Fry, W.E. 1982. *Principles of plant disease management.* London: Academic Press.

Game Conservancy, 1992. *Guidelines 1992/93: management of Conservation Headlands.* Fordingbridge: Game Conservancy.

Gibson, C.W.D. & Brown, V.K. 1991. The effects of grazing on local colonization and extinction during early succession. *Journal of Vegetation Science*, **2**, 291–300.

Jones, N.E. & Naylor, R.E.L. 1992. The significance of the seed rain from set-aside. In: *Set-aside*, edited by J. Clarke, 91–96. Farnham: British Crop Protection Council.

Osborne, P. 1989. *The management of set-aside land for birds: a practical guide.* Sandy: Royal Society for the Protection of Birds.

Parr, T.W. & Way, J.M. 1988. Management of roadside vegetation: the long-term effects of cutting. *Journal of Applied Ecology,* **25**, 1073–1087.

Smith, H. & Macdonald, D.W. 1992. The impacts of mowing and sowing on weed populations and species richness in field margin set-aside. In: *Set-aside*, edited by J. Clarke, 117–122. Farnham: British Crop Protection Council.

Sotherton, N.W., Boatman, N.D. & Robertson, P.A. 1992. The use of set-aside land for game conservation. In: *Set-aside*, edited by J. Clarke, 223–228. Farnham: British Crop Protection Council.

Wilson, P.J. 1992. The natural regeneration of vegetation under set-aside in southern England. In: *Set-aside*, edited by J. Clarke, 73–78. Farnham: British Crop Protection Council.

Yarham, D.J. & Symonds, B.V. 1992. Effects of set-aside on diseases of cereals. In: *Set-aside*, edited by J. Clarke, 41–46. Farnham: British Crop Protection Council.

9 BRENT GEESE PASTURE

Summary

Brent geese will feed on open, undisturbed fields with short, fertile swards near to coastal roosts. Such sites will divert them from feeding on nearby crops.

Introduction

Numbers of dark-bellied Brent geese (*Branta bernicla bernicla*) were restricted to some 15 000 in the 1950s, but now are estimated to exceed 200 000. Around half of these birds overwinter in Britain, mostly in the south-east of England. The species is noted in the EC Birds Directive (Commission of the European Communities 1979), and so Britain has a particular responsibility for the conservation of this species. The problem is that these birds have switched from feeding entirely on intertidal mudflats and salt marshes to feeding inland on grass and arable crops. They can cause yield losses of between 6–10% on winter wheat (Summers 1990), and so are now regarded as agricultural pests in some areas of the U.K.

Field selection appears to be on the basis of the percentage of live grass in the sward, and fields with short, thistle-free swards appear to be favoured (Summers & Critchley 1990). Therefore, it is possible to attract geese from arable land to alternative feeding areas (Vickery & Summers 1992).

This possibility was explored within an option under the Countryside Premium Scheme for Brent geese pasture (Countryside Commission 1991). The progress of this option was reviewed by Vickery and Sutherland (1992), who observed that over 50% of the fields established in 1988–89 were actually used by the geese in 1992. The selected fields had significantly shorter swards than those not used. They presented additional evidence suggesting that a properly located and managed sward can be very attractive to the geese, and that, by attracting geese from nearby arable land, savings of up to £100 ha^{-1} of set-aside could accrue. Grazing areas can be created on non-rotational set-aside land, but an exemption is needed because of the requirement to apply fertilizer.

These guidelines can be readily adapted for winter feeding areas for other geese if desired, but the management of the sward height may need to be modified.

Criteria for site selection

Summers and Critchley (1990) suggest that sites should be no more than 1 km inland, and no more than 4–5 km from night roosts on coastal salt marshes. The Countryside Premium Scheme used a limit of nearly 5 km (3 miles) from the sea (Countryside Commission 1991), and Vickery and Sutherland (1992) found that use of these sites by the geese was not influenced by distance from sea or roost sites. Sites should, therefore, be located within 1 km of roosting sites, unless there is evidence of local feeding on crops.

Information necessary to identify and define suitable sites

Target habitat	Short-sward, nutrient-rich grassland.
Location of site	One km from the sea (5 km at most), adjacent to salt marsh areas frequented by Brent geese around the southern and eastern coasts from Lincoln to Dorset (Summers & Critchley 1990).
Location of site in relation to target habitat distribution	Not applicable.

Information necessary to assess the suitability of the site for restoration to the target habitat type

Any arable land in the correct location should be suitable.

Size	The site should be at least 5 ha and in an open situation. Ideally, several fields should be available.
Soils	Not relevant.
Recent management history	Not relevant.
Management on adjacent land	The birds are prone to move to alternative feeding sites when disturbed (Summers & Critchley 1990). Therefore, alternative sites should be available; the Countryside Premium Scheme recommends the use of three sites at least 500 m apart – if they are any closer, all sites may be affected by the same disturbance. Sites particularly prone to disturbance should not be used.
Proximity to existing habitat	Not applicable, but the sites should be within 3 miles of salt marsh roosting sites.

Checklist of additional features
None

Other designations/schemes
Twelve sites were entered for the Countryside Premium Scheme (Vickery & Sutherland 1992).

Management

The guidelines adopted by the Countryside Premium Scheme (Countryside Commission 1991) have been successful whenever the sward height was less than 6–7 cm in January, achieved by ensuring that sward height in September was kept below 5 cm. Otherwise, experimental comparisons showed that the exact details of the cutting and grazing regimes had little effect after the first year, although the application of nitrogen fertilizer at 50 kg N ha^{-1} did increase grazing densities (Vickery & Sutherland 1992).

Year 1

Establish a grass sward using a mixture of perennial rye-grass (*Lolium perenne* late-heading variety, eg Melle, Wendy), white clover (*Trifolium repens*) and timothy (*Phleum pratense*) in the proportions 5:1:1 sown at a rate of 30 kg ha^{-1}. Up to 5% creeping red fescue (*Festuca rubra rubra*) may be included. It may be necessary to discourage wildfowl while this sward establishes. Apply nitrogen in organic or inorganic form at a rate of 50 kg ha^{-1} between 15 August and 30 September.

Subsequent years

Apply nitrogen in organic or inorganic form at a maximum rate of 50 kg ha^{-1} in late September or October; leave the edge of the field unfertilized. Cut the sward to no more than 5 cm in height between June and October; at least twice in Year 2 and subsequent years, ensuring a sward height of 5 cm at most in late September–October. Too few cuts would damage the sward because of the amount of cuttings; four or more cuts may be needed where there is no autumn grazing. Weeds should not be allowed to dominate.

Aim of management

To produce a short, nutrient-rich grass sward.

Site preparation techniques (if any)

Not applicable.

Options for follow-up management

Not applicable.

Financial implications (capital and recurrent costs)

There are costs of establishment and management. However, there are also gains in diverting geese from crops, which could exceed £100 ha^{-1} (Vickery & Sutherland 1992).

Potential off-site implications of different options

Diversion of feeding flocks from crops.

Procedures and problems encountered for return to arable land

There may be substantial nitrate leaching if the land is ploughed.

Additional on-site implications of management
Management is compatible with autumn sheep or cattle grazing (Vickery & Sutherland 1992).

Timescales
Grazing by geese should begin in the second winter, and should continue indefinitely.

Potentially damaging operations
Possible damaging operations include allowing the sward height to exceed 7 cm in January, and excessive disturbance.

Appraisal

If successful, the field should host Brent geese (detectable by droppings as well as by sight) in the second and subsequent winters.

Potential off-site impacts

Reduced grazing on neighbouring arable land. Potential for nitrate runoff.

Implications for access

While there is no need to prevent access entirely, provided other sites are available nearby, it should be discouraged.

References

Countryside Commission. 1991. *The countryside premium for set-aside land.* Cambridge: Countryside Commission.

Commission of the European Communities. 1979. Council Directive 79/409/EEC of 2 April 1979 on the conservation of wild birds. *Official Journal of the European Communities*, L 103.

Summers, R.W. 1990. The effect on winter wheat of grazing by Brent geese *Branta bernicla*. *Journal of Applied Ecology*, **27**, 821–833.

Summers, R.W. & Critchley, C.N.R. 1990. Use of grassland and field selection by Brent geese *Branta bernicla*. *Journal of Applied Ecology*, **27**, 834–846.

Vickery, J.A. & Summers, R.W. 1992. Cost-effectiveness of scaring Brent geese *Branta b. bernicla* from fields of arable crops by a human scarer. *Crop Protection*, **11**, 480–484.

Vickery, J.A. & Sutherland, W.J. 1992. Brent geese: a conflict between conservation and agriculture. In: *Set-aside*, edited by J. Clarke, 187–193. Farnham: British Crop Protection Council.

10 STONE CURLEW MEADOW

Summary

Stone curlews are rare, site-faithful birds requiring large areas with a mix of grassland and regularly disturbed or very open vegetation.

Introduction

The stone curlew (*Burhinus oedicnemus*) is a rare summer visitor, whose range is from Britain to southern Russia, and south to southern France, Italy, the Balkans and the Caucasus. Its range in Britain is contracting; it was formerly widespread as far north as Yorkshire, but now is restricted to south-east from a line between the Wash and Dorset. Its numbers are declining too, and are now below 150 pairs a year (Batten *et al.* 1990).

It breeds on open, stony ground with short or sparse vegetation; suitable habitats include semi-natural grassland if intensively grazed by sheep or rabbits (*Oryctolagus cuniculus*), chalk downland, Breckland heaths and arable land. The birds tend to return to previous nesting sites. Eggs are laid from April to August: typically two eggs per clutch, and sometimes two clutches per year. The birds feed on invertebrates and occasional small mammals and birds, taken from tightly grazed semi-natural and improved grassland, pig fields, manured arable land, arable field margins and manure heaps. The birds will feed 2–3 km away from the nest.

Numbers of stone curlew are declining because of the loss of tightly grazed grassland, through conversion to arable and the relaxation of grazing by rabbits and sheep, and changes in the management of arable land making the cover too dense for the birds, even in more open crops such as sugar beet. Mechanical operations, increases in foxes (*Vulpes vulpes*), disturbance (even from bird watchers) and egg collectors are additional problems for the species.

The management procedures are taken from the wildlife fallow recommendations of the Royal Society for the Protection of Birds (RSPB) (Osborne 1989) and the Countryside Commission (Countryside Commission 1991), and are similar to the annually tilled non-rotational natural regeneration and sown cover scheme (Chapter 8). An exemption is needed for the spring tillage treatment.

Criteria for site selection

The ideal sites are ones which already support breeding stone curlews. Sites close to present sites which have had stone curlews in the past should also be considered.

Information necessary to identify and define suitable sites

Target habitat | Sparsely vegetated light soils, with short grassland nearby.

Location of site | Stone curlews are now found in the Breckland, Hampshire and Dorset, although they have nested in other areas in the south-east in the past. Details can be supplied by the British Trust for Ornithology and the RSPB.

Location of site in relation to target habitat distribution | Not applicable.

Information necessary to assess the suitability of the site for restoration to the target habitat type

Size | Stone curlews seek areas with good visibility of at least 1 ha (preferably 2 ha), ideally square, with a lowest dimension of 50 m (preferably 100 m).

Soils	Soils are typically light, sandy and/or stony over a chalk substrate.
Recent management history	If stone curlews are already breeding at the site, previous management is irrelevant. In other cases, there is unlikely to be a problem, unless there has been a build-up of soil fertility encouraging the rapid growth of weeds.
Management on adjacent land	If there is no short grassland planned within the field itself, it should be available within 1–2 km.
Proximity to existing habitat	Sites should already have breeding stone curlews, or have had them in the past.

Checklist of additional features

Sites should have an open aspect, and not be surrounded by tall vegetation.

Other designations/schemes

This option is compatible with the Breckland Environmentally Sensitive Area, and possibly Site of Special Scientific Interest management agreements.

Management

Stone curlews are site-faithful, and need a mosaic of sparse vegetation and dense grassland. The sparse vegetation is maintained simply by discing to a depth of 8 cm in early spring (no later than March), cutting the vegetation just beforehand if necessary. An exemption to the set-aside rules is required. Grass areas can be managed according to the meadow strip/chalk grassland options (Chapters 6 & 8), providing disturbance is minimised during spring and early summer.

Aim of management

To maintain areas of sparse vegetation alongside grassland over long periods of time.

Site preparation techniques (if any)

Plan the areas to be kept sparse and to be grassed over. Ideally, they should be part of the same field, if the field is large enough, with the sparse area towards the centre of the field. If there is well-established close-cropped grassland nearby, the whole field should be managed for sparse vegetation. In the autumn after cropping, allow natural regeneration in the sparse area. The grassed area can be developed either from natural regeneration (if the land has recently been converted from grassland) or by sowing (Chapters 6 & 8). If weeds become a problem, spot treatment of herbicides may be needed, but, because of the risk of disturbing the birds, treatment should be as late as possible and even then only when strictly necessary.

Options for follow-up management

The grassed areas can be converted to lightly grazed swards, and used to recreate sandy or chalk grasslands.

Financial implications (capital and recurrent costs)

Management costs of the sparse areas are low – one cultivation and one cut per year, but the management of the grassed areas may involve sowing seeds and additional mowing.

Potential off-site implications of different options

None.

Procedures and problems encountered for return to arable land

There are none, although suitable land is likely to be marginal for arable agriculture anyway.

Additional on-site implications of management

Other birds such as lapwings (*Vanellus vanellus*), skylarks (*Alauda arvensis*), thrushes, finches and buntings will also use the fields. Any spring-germinating rare arable weeds will flourish, as will insects.

Timescales

Sparse areas should be acceptable to the birds in the first season;

grassed areas may require longer. Once birds are using the areas, management should be continued for as long as possible.

Potentially damaging operations

Herbicides and pesticides should not be applied to nesting or feeding areas, except for selective/spot treatment of some grass weed species.

Appraisal

The site should be home to stone curlews. Increases in other birds and rare weeds (Table 1) can be used to indicate benefits to other wildlife.

Potential off-site impacts

None.

Implications for access

Access should be minimised between 1 April and 31 July each year. A system of hides may be desired for public viewing of the birds.

References

Batten, L.A., Bibby, C.J., Clement, P., Elliott, G.D. & Porter, R.F. 1990. *Red Data birds in Britain, action for rare, threatened and important species.* London: Poyser.

Countryside Commission. 1991. *The countryside premium for set-aside land.* Cambridge: Countryside Commission.

Osborne, P. 1989. *The management of set-aside land for birds: a practical guide.* Sandy: Royal Society for the Protection of Birds.

LONGER-TERM HABITAT RESTORATION USING SET-ASIDE LAND

The non-rotational set-aside programme involves a commitment for five years, in which time great benefits to wildlife can be achieved. Some of the habitats created under this scheme may well be of particular value, either for wildlife or for public access, and so may be retained. However, some habitat restoration projects are intrinsically longer term in nature. They can be started under non-rotational set-aside, but substantial benefits may take several years to accrue. These projects are more appropriate to the proposed longer-term Habitat Scheme.

Here, we give four example options. Damp grassland is one option already specified under the non-rotational set-aside scheme, and salt marsh restoration is expected to be an option under the 1994 Habitat Scheme. We also include suggestions for calcareous grassland and we consider sandy grassland and lowland heath restoration together. These proposals assume that the land can be entered into the set-aside scheme, and so are more restrictive than would be the case if the land were to be entered solely for the Habitat Scheme, for which the set-aside rules do not apply.

11 CALCAREOUS GRASSLAND

Summary

Calcareous grassland is of prime conservation importance for scarce plants. It can only be restored on suitable soils, and should ideally be adjacent to existing calcareous grassland or on land only recently converted from calcareous grassland. Restoration involves sowing a suitable seed mixture and regular mowing and/or grazing (within the rules of the chosen scheme). The rate of immigration of plant species varies greatly, but some species are very slow and may never appear unless sown.

Introduction

Calcareous grassland is distributed over a variety of geological formations, which are chemically all limestones, ranging from the soft Cretaceous chalk through the moderately hard Oolitic (Jurassic) series to the hard rock of the Carboniferous. Calcareous grassland is also found on limestone with large amounts of magnesium and on calcareous igneous and metamorphic rocks, including pumice tiff, dolerite, basalt, andesite and certain schists and gneisses.

Related communities are also found on soils derived from sand and chalky boulder clays in Breckland and elsewhere.

The soils derived from these different parent materials are relatively similar chemically, and it is this common factor which gives the characteristic composition, both in terms of floristics and structure, to calcareous grasslands – habitats uniquely rich in terms of numbers and conservation value of plant species (eg Lousley 1950). Grassland restored on set-aside land cannot possibly match ancient chalk grasslands in species richness, but it will benefit the more common species and can provide an invaluable buffer area around existing well-established habitat.

Criteria for site selection

It would be possible to develop selection rules based on soil type, proximity to suitable habitat, and (if desired) management history.

Information necessary to identify and define suitable sites

Target habitat   Calcareous grassland.

Location of site   The site should occur in a region which is known to be associated with geological formations which give rise to calcareous soils, eg the South Downs, in the Chiltern Hills, and in south-west Wiltshire.

Location of site in relation to target habitat distribution   There is no national map showing the distribution of calcareous grassland, although the information is probably available for most areas at a county level. As a starting point, the site should be located on the geological map of Great Britain (scale 1:625 000) to see if it occurs on formations which *may* give rise to calcareous soils, bearing in mind the fact that superficial deposits may mask the calcareous nature of the underlying rock. The site should also be located on the Soil Map of England and Wales (scale 1:1 000 000); larger-scale soil maps are available for some regions, and should be consulted when available.

Information on the distribution of calcareous grasslands on a county or regional basis is often available, although not usually in a published form. Both English Nature and the local County Wildlife Trusts have this information; for some counties, eg Bedfordshire, it is available on 6" maps, although the Wildlife Trusts will make a charge for access to their data.

Size

Calcareous grasslands can be created on small sites. For example, ITE has within a ten-year period produced a grassland containing five grasses and 28 forbs in plots 5 m x 2 m situated on ex-arable chalk soils at Royston. While small areas are known to support a rich flora, little is known about the minimum areas required for supporting the fauna associated with calcareous grasslands.

Soils

The soil type is the crucial factor in creating calcareous grasslands. Soils should be derived from calcareous rocks (Chalk, Oolitic, Carboniferous or Magnesium limestone in the main, or from chalky boulder clay). In many cases, they will be rendzinas or brown calcimorphic soils. They will be characterised by a high pH (usually in the range 5.5–8.4), a high available calcium ion content (usually in the range 300–1000 mg Ca 100 g^{-1}), a high free calcium carbonate content (30–75%) and often with a high organic matter content (7–20%). They may contain a proportion of flints or gravel. They will be well drained and, except for boulder clays, will not suffer from waterlogging. They are likely to have considerable amounts of nitrogen and phosphorus in the top 20 cm, especially if they have been used previously for growing grain crops.

Recent management history

From the point of view of trying to establish calcareous grassland, it matters little if the land use for the past five years has been intensive arable, intensive grass or leys alternating with arable. The fact that the land has been used for *intensive* agriculture means that soil nutrient status will be high, and that other agrochemicals, such as herbicides and insecticides, will have also been used. Under these conditions, the seed bank of calcareous grassland species will have been totally depleted, although certain arable weeds will have survived (Graham & Hutchings 1988a,b).

Previous crop yield (especially in the last year) will provide an excellent indication of the nutrient status of the site – the lower the yield, the less fertile the site, and the easier it will be to establish calcareous grassland. This is probably a better guide to the potential of a site for habitat restoration than knowing the previous fertilizer inputs.

Results from long-term ITE experiments conducted by T C E Wells at Royston, Herts (established 1973), and the Great Chishill experiment (established 1986) indicate that 'nutrient draining' techniques are not required on chalk soils as a prerequisite for establishing calcareous grasslands, provided that seed of calcareous grassland species is sown and no reliance is placed on seed in the soil seed bank.

Management of adjacent land

Every effort should be made to ensure that spray drift from adjacent arable or grassland is prevented or kept to a minimum. The same principle applies to applications of inorganic fertilizers and the deposition of organic manures from intensively housed livestock. Any 'accidental' input of nitrogenous fertilizer will encourage coarse grasses at the expense of low-growing forbs. Because of the risk of NO_x and NH_3 compounds derived from livestock reaching newly created grasslands, intensive livestock should not be kept nearby.

Proximity to existing habitats

Best results will be achieved if the set-aside is immediately adjacent to existing grassland: the greater the distance away, the less chance of a species colonising. Research on colonisation of chalk grassland (eg Hope-Simpson 1940; Cornish 1954; Wells *et al.* 1976; Gibson, Watt & Brown 1987; Gibson & Brown 1991; Graham & Hutchings 1988b) has concentrated on low-fertility sites surrounded by mature grassland. Grass seed is mostly heavy and will blow a few metres and gradually invade a site, but progress is slow. Where new sites are separated from existing grassland by more than 200 m, colonisation may take years or even decades for most species. Sites 1 km or more from existing species-rich grassland are unlikely to be reached by calcareous grassland species for many years.

Sites more isolated from existing chalk grasslands can still be used, but here the species composition will reflect almost exclusively the species sown into the area and any surviving arable weeds and other species already in the seed bank.

Checklist of additional features
Not applicable.

Other designations/schemes
The Environmentally Sensitive Area scheme (ESAs) makes specific reference to the creation of chalk grassland and the management of

existing grassland if it occurs within the designated area. At present, such grassland is found within the following ESAs: South Downs, Cotswold Hills, Hampshire Avon Valley, North Dorset/South Wilts Downs and possibly within the North West Kent Coast.

There is also a chalk grassland option under the Countryside Stewardship Scheme, and this option is consistent with the Nitrate Sensitive Areas scheme.

Management

There is scope for allowing natural regeneration in situations where chalk grassland has existed until very recently and is adjacent to remaining chalk grassland. It should be managed by cutting in the same way as a planted sward. However, in the vast majority of cases, the grassland species will have to be sown.

Aim of management
The aim of management is to create a facsimile of calcareous grassland. The communities which should be used as 'models' can be defined in terms of phytosociological units or in the National Vegetation Classification (NVC) categories. For example, in the case of chalk grasslands, we would be aiming at creating some type of Mesobromion grassland. In NVC terms (Rodwell 1992), we might be aiming for CG2, CG3 or CG5.

Site preparation techniques
The key to the establishment of wild flower mixtures from seed is attention to four points:

* selection of species suitable for site conditions
* a weed-free seed bed
* careful seed bed preparation
* careful management of the site, especially in the first year after sowing.

Where weeds are present, they should be eliminated with a herbicide such as glyphosate. A fine seed bed with a good tilth should be prepared, as the seed of many wild flower species is small. It is a fallacy that wild flower mixtures can be sown in rough seed beds, and a common fault with them is that they are too loose and uneven. A firm bed can be achieved by repeated harrowing and rolling, the timing of these operations in respect of the weather being crucial to the result obtained: wet conditions should be avoided.

On small areas, seed will normally be sown by hand, but on larger areas it may be applied by tractor-mounted seed or fertilizer broadcasters. The grass and wild flower mixture is usually sown at about 2.5 g m^{-2}. If desired, it can be sown with a nurse crop, such as Westerwolds rye-grass at 3–4.5 g m^{-2}; this must be cut before it can shed seed, and will disappear within two years (Wells 1991). A suitable seed mixture is shown in Table 2; it should be regarded as being typical rather than definitive, as seed mixes should reflect local variation in grassland communities.

The best time for sowing wild flower mixtures is from the end of August to mid-September, but good results have been obtained at other times in those parts of the country where rain is plentiful throughout the year.

Follow-up management

Management during the first two years is crucial both to the establishment and to the final composition of the sward. It is difficult to make hard and fast rules as each site is different, but generally the newly sown area may require cutting at least three times in the first year after sowing, removing the cut material each time to prevent smothering and to reduce nutrient levels (an exemption to the set-aside rules will be needed). Timing of the cuts will depend on the stage of growth of the sown vegetation and any weeds. As a rule-of-thumb, cut when the height exceeds about 15 cm.

After the first year, management will depend on the site's fertility, the type of mixture sown, and the effect required. In general, the more fertile the site, the greater will be the need for management. Where mixtures are composed of tall and medium-tall herbs and grasses, they should be cut in late July or early August and again in late

October or early November. Where mixtures largely comprise short-growing plants, a single late cut will suffice. The cut material should be removed, but this will require an exemption. On large areas, some form of rotational management will be beneficial.

Some species are expensive as seed, or do not establish well when sown. These can be introduced as pot-grown plants after the first year of the grassland; examples include quaking grass (*Briza media*), clustered bellflower (*Campanula glomerata*), harebell (*C. rotundifolia*), horse-shoe vetch (*Hippocrepis comosa*) and larger wild thyme (*Thymus pulegioides)* (Wells 1991).

Extensive sheep grazing regimes can be applied to improve the diversity of the maturing grassland (Gibson, Watt & Brown 1987); this is possible in the autumn under set-aside and all year round if the land is entered just for the Habitat Scheme.

Financial implications
Assuming that the farm has the usual range of tractors and other machinery, there will be no capital cost except for purchasing the seeds mixture. The cost of the seeds mixture will depend on its composition. A species-rich mixture, with eight grasses and 25 forbs will cost between £700 and £1,000 ha^{-1}. A mixture containing only two or three grasses and up to five forbs may be obtained for as little as £200 ha^{-1}.

The recurrent costs will mostly be concerned with management and will depend on whether the site requires mowing once or three times a year. If cut material is removed, as is recommended, then the cost of forage harvesting must be taken into account.

Potential off-site implications of different options
None.

Procedures and problems encountered for return to arable land
The land can simply be ploughed up and managed as normal.

Additional on-site implications of management

Populations of hares (*Lepus europaeus*), insects and birds should all increase.

Timescales

Five years is required for a range of plant species to establish and give the appearance of calcareous grassland. For the species composition to begin to approach that of mature calcareous grassland, a period of 10–15 years is required.

Gibson and Brown (1991) categorise a range of chalk grassland species according to their appearance within stands of different ages. Weeds and coarse grasses are common initially, but become sparse in older grassland (over ten years). Mid-successional species (defined as 11–100 years) should appear within 20 years or so, whereas consitituents of older grassland may appear within this time if they are present in adjacent land. Their species lists broadly agree with results from ITE experiments.

Some species are highly unlikely ever to appear; for example, there is no evidence from historical studies that species such as the pasque flower *(Pulsatilla vulgaris)* and the spotted cat's-ear (*Hypochaeris maculata*) ever colonise new sites, despite both species producing fertile seed and the latter species having an achene fruit with a parachute mechanism. Other species, such as the horse-shoe vetch, have indehiscent pods with no known dispersal mechanism. In ITE experiments on Royston Heath, this species is still confined to the plots it was planted in after 18 years.

Potentially damaging operations

Any application of artificial fertilizers or herbicides will damage the developing grassland.

Cutting the sward at the wrong time of the year can eliminate species which require annual or biennial replacement. For example, yellow-rattle (*Rhinanthus minor*) and wild carrot (*Daucus carota*) will be eliminated from the sward if cutting occurs before seed has fallen in late June.

Appraisal

Criteria for judging the success or failure of habitat restoration on set-aside land should include the following.

- The establishment of characteristic calcareous grassland species. If the site was sown with a seeds mixture, some arbitrary value should be established, eg >50% of sown species to establish in three years. Sampling should reflect the sowing densities used.

- Cycling of species within the sward. This infers that successful species will flower and set seed, and also that suitable conditions for re-establishment are provided.

- The absence of a high proportion of aggressive weeds, such as creeping thistle (*Cirsium arvense*), broad-leaved dock (*Rumex obtusifolius*) and spear thistle (*Cirsium vulgare*), in the sward. Again, this could be quantified on a percentage basis, eg <10% cover of such species.

- The presence of at least some invertebrates associated with calcareous grassland, eg common blue butterfly (*Polyommatus icarus*).

- The absence of a large number of arable weeds by the second year in sown swards.

All the following plants should be present after 20 years, and assessment after ten years may be based on the proportion of these species which can be found.

Yarrow	*Achillea millefolium*
Oat-grass	*Arrhenatherum elatius*
Daisy	*Bellis perennis*
Slender false-brome	*Brachypodium sylvaticum*
Lesser knapweed	*Centaurea nigra*
Greater knapweed	*Centaurea scabiosa*
Wild basil	*Clinopodium vulgare*
Cock's-foot	*Dactylis glomerata*
Red fescue	*Festuca rubra*

Cow parsnip	*Heracleum sphondylium*
Common St John's wort	*Hypericum perforatum*
Ox-eye daisy	*Leucanthemum vulgare*
Restharrow	*Ononis repens*
Wild parsnip	*Pastinaca sativa*
Ribwort	*Plantago lanceolata*
Narrow-leaved meadow-grass	*Poa angustifolia*
Bulbous buttercup	*Ranunculus bulbosus*
Hoary ragwort	*Senecio erucifolius*
Red clover	*Trifolium pratense*
Tufted vetch	*Vicia cracca*

Potential off-site impacts

Rabbits may increase, along with some aphids.

Access

There are no restrictions, except that trampling should be avoided while new grassland is establishing in the first year. Entry into the Countryside Access Scheme can be considered.

Table 2. Grass/forb mixture suitable for creating a chalk or limestone grassland
(source: Wells 1991)

Grasses Common name	Latin name	% by weight of grasses	kg ha^{-1}
Upright brome	*Bromus erectus*	10	2.4
Crested dog's tail	*Cynosurus cristatus*	15	3.6
Sheep's fescue	*Festuca ovina*	25	6.0
Red fescue	*Festuca rubra pruinosa*	20	4.8
Meadow oat	*Helictotrichon pratense*	5	1.2
Crested hair-grass	*Koeleria cristata*	5	1.2
Smooth-stalked meadow-grass	*Poa pratensis angustifolia*	10	2.4
Yellow oat	*Trisetum flavescens*	10	2.4
	Total	100	24.0

Forbs Common name	Latin name	% by weight of forbs	kg ha^{-1}
Yarrow	*Achillea millefolium*	4	240
Kidney-vetch	*Anthyllis vulneraria*	4	240
Lesser knapweed	*Centaurea nigra*	5	300
Greater knapweed	*C. scabiosa*	2	120
Wild basil	*Clinopodium vulgare*	2	120
Dropwort	*Filipendula vulgaris*	2	120
Lady's bedstraw	*Galium verum*	3	180
Rough hawkbit	*Leontodon hispidus*	2	120
Ox-eye daisy	*Leucanthemum vulgare*	15	900
Birdsfoot-trefoil	*Lotus corniculatus*	2	120
Black medick	*Medicago lupulina*	2	120
Sainfoin	*Onobrychis viciifolia*	5	300
Burnet saxifrage	*Pimpinella saxifraga*	1	60
Ribwort	*Plantago lanceolata*	5	300
Hoary plantain	*P. media*	5	300
Cowslip	*Primula veris*	4	240
Self-heal	*Prunella vulgaris*	10	600
Bulbous buttercup	*Ranunculus bulbosus*	2	120
Wild mignonette	*Reseda lutea*	4	240
Yellow-rattle	*Rhinanthus minor*	10	600
Salad burnet	*Sanguisorba minor*	4	240
Bladder campion	*Silene vulgaris*	1	60
Betony	*Stachys officinalis*	2	120
	Total	100	6000

References

Cornish, M.W. 1954. The origin and structure of the grassland types of the central North Downs. *Journal of Ecology*, **42**, 359–374.

Gibson, C.W.D. & Brown, V.K. 1991. The nature and rate of development of calcareous grassland in southern Britain. *Biological Conservation*, **58**, 297–316.

Gibson, C.W.D., Watt, T.A. & Brown, V.K. 1987. The use of sheep grazing to recreate species-rich grassland from abandoned arable land. *Biological Conservation*, **42**, 165–183.

Graham, D.J. & Hutchings, M.J. 1988a. Estimation of the seed bank of a chalk grassland ley established on former arable land. *Journal of Applied Ecology*, **25**, 253–263.

Graham, D.J. & Hutchings, M.J. 1988b. A field investigation of germination from the seed bank of a chalk grassland ley on former arable land. *Journal of Applied Ecology*, **25**, 253–263.

Hope-Simpson, J.F. 1940. Studies of the vegetation of the English chalk. VI: Late stages in succession leading to chalk grassland. *Journal of Ecology*, **28**, 386–402.

Lousley, J.E. 1950. *Wild flowers of chalk and limestone.* London: Collins.

Rodwell, J.S., ed. 1992. *Grasslands and montane communities.* Cambridge: Cambridge University Press.

Wells, T.C.E. 1991. Restoring and re-creating species-rich lowland dry grassland. In: *The conservation of lowland dry grassland birds in Europe*, edited by P.D. Goriup, L.A. Batten & J.A. Norton, 125–132. Peterborough: Joint Nature Conservation Committee.

Wells, T.C.E., Sheail, J., Ball, D.F. & Ward, L.K. 1976. Ecological studies on the Porton Ranges: relationship between vegetation, soils and land use history. *Journal of Ecology*, **64**, 589–626.

12 DAMP GRASSLAND

Summary

Damp lowland meadows can be restored in suitable areas, eg floodplains and the Fens, sometimes simply by allowing the water table to rise. They have prime conservation importance for wading and other birds, even where it is difficult to recreate the plant communities typical of unimproved damp grassland.

Introduction

The loss of unimproved damp pastures because of drainage and fertilization has been well recorded (eg Fuller 1987). However, the ITE analysis of species declines (Firbank *et al.* 1992) suggested that losses of scarce plants were modest compared with some other habitats. The ITE study looked at presence and absence in 10 km squares, and so declines in abundance at more local levels could not be detected. The implication is that the species characteristic of unimproved pasture may remain widely distributed, even though they may be restricted to small patches at a given locality. There is, therefore, scope to use set-aside to extend these small patches as a basis for restoring this habitat; such newly restored damp grasslands will then be readily colonised by waders and other animals which have declined as a result of habitat loss.

Set-aside for upland damp grassland differs from that for lowlands, in that sheep grazing is believed to be an essential component if the target habitat is to be created and maintained. Grazing is only permitted in the autumn under non-rotational set-aside, and research is needed to show how such limited grazing can be complemented or replaced by cutting and mowing regimes; experience from lowland situations may be a useful initial guide. The upland grassland habitat has attracted little attention from conservationists, but is very important for some of our wading birds. There is evidence of local losses in this habitat, and also of local turnover – grassland being lost to improved grassland, but being replenished from other habitats (Buse 1992).

Criteria for site selection

Sites for the restoration of wet grassland should ideally be in areas where this habitat was converted to arable during the period from 1945 onward, the more recently the better. Although restoration may be most desirable in the largely arable areas in east England (eg the Fenland basin and Humberhead Levels), such areas may have been too grossly modified to allow successful restoration as isolated pockets within areas of intensive agriculture. Selected sites will be concentrated in coastal levels, the floodplains of major rivers, and areas with gentle topography on soils with impeded drainage.

Information necessary to identify and define suitable sites

Target habitat   Species-rich, wet, mesotrophic grassland.

Location of site   Suitable sites may be found anywhere, but particularly on flat, gently sloping or undulating land at low altitudes with problems of surface or groundwater drainage.

Location of site in relation to target habitat distribution   Successful restoration is most likely on clays and loams, of mildly acidic to neutral reaction, in the lowlands of England and Wales. Some of the unimproved, mesotrophic grassland that has survived is in this zone (Fuller 1987). Species typical of old grassland spread primarily by vegetative means, and proximity to existing target habitat cannot be relied upon to provide a seed source for the natural colonisation of set-aside land. However, seed mixtures derived from existing old grasslands may be sown on nearby set-aside fields.

Information necessary to assess the suitability of the site for restoration to the target habitat type

Many sites will be unsuitable for restoring to wet mesotrophic grassland because the soils are naturally too free-draining and have no historic need for groundwater control. Second, separate control of groundwater in the set-aside land may be too expensive or complex in the context of the surrounding intensively farmed land.

Size	Most sizes of site are suitable although, because these grasslands require mowing, the type of equipment available for this management may be used most effectively on larger sites. Similarly, where groundwater control is required, it will be more practical where large areas are managed.
Soils	Establishment will be most successful on surface water gley, groundwater gley and peat soils. However, where the structure of the peat has been destroyed through drainage and oxidation, wetting up of the soil may be unsuccessful. Soil fertility should ideally be low to moderate, ie sufficiently high to allow establishment of a range of grasses and forbs, but not so high that the sward becomes dominated by species that demand a high nitrogen status, eg Yorkshire fog (*Holcus lanatus*), perennial rye-grass (*Lolium perenne*) and timothy (*Phleum pratense*).
Recent management history	Although wet grassland may be established in most sites where the soil type is suitable, ideally the site should have a short history of arable use, with evidence that the land was previously managed as hay meadow or pasture. However, the seed bank under arable land is poor in species characteristic of wet mesotrophic swards, and regeneration

from that source cannot be relied upon. If
sowing a wild flower mixture is planned,
some attempt to adjust soil fertility may be
necessary. Sites where fertilizer and
herbicide inputs have been low will be most
suitable. Any past attempt to improve the
drainage may have to be negated.

**Management on
adjacent land**

Establishment will be most successful where
the neighbouring land is neither
underdrained nor subject to pump drainage.
Wet grassland can be established in sites
within a matrix of drained land, but success
could require the hydrological isolation of
the set-aside land.

**Proximity to existing
habitat**

Unless the existing habitat directly abuts the
set-aside land and allows vegetative spread,
recruitment may rely on the provision of
seed from further afield. Therefore, existing
habitat need not be present locally, though
the most appropriate seed mixture for
sowing on the set-aside may be harvested
from nearby existing habitats on the same
soil type. Damp grassland will provide an
excellent buffer for fenland and other
wetland habitats.

Checklist of additional features
None.

Other designations/schemes
Attempts to restore old wet grassland are also being made either
within the context of Environmentally Sensitive Area (ESA) legislation
(particularly Tiers 2 and 3) and the Countryside Stewardship
Scheme. Such schemes normally begin from improved, permanent
grassland rather than from arable land.

Management

Management options will depend upon the duration of the proposed set-aside, the suitability of the soil water regime and fertility, and the proximity of existing habitat. Wet mesotrophic grassland should not be considered for short-term or rotational set-aside.

Wet grassland restoration should begin by allowing natural regeneration after harvest. Those species which colonise should be identified and the correspondence of the vegetation to the composition of the target habitat assessed.

If the sward which develops naturally is floristically close to wet mesotrophic grassland (and at least some relevant species can persist in the seed bank for many years, notably rushes and sedges), subsequent management may be confined to annual mowing in July combined with the removal of the cuttings (an exemption is required). This practice will reduce soil fertility and suppress those species which demand a high nitrogen status.

Suitable successions may take place where existing habitat is directly adjacent to the set-aside land or where damp grassland species have persisted in the seed bank. At many sites, however, set-aside will result in a coarse grass sward with only a small wetland component. In such cases, following a year (or more) of fallow with an annual hay cut, the site should be ploughed and harrowed to produce a seed bed. Seed derived from wet mesotrophic grasslands may then be broadcast in the autumn. Alternatively, hay harvested from existing habitat may be strewn over the field in autumn.

After sowing, the subsequent growth should be mown to 7.5 cm in the spring following the autumn sowing and, if possible, the mowing should be repeated in that year whenever the sward height exceeds 20 cm, to reduce fertility and suppress weeds and aggressive grasses. Some spot treatment of notifiable weeds with herbicide may be countenanced, but should usually be discouraged.

Following the development of a wet mesotrophic sward, autumn grazing should be considered. This will provide mosaics of tussocks and short swards valuable for many insects, and depressions (footprints) will be used by breeding birds. If the characteristic wetland species decline and are replaced by species of more freely drained sites, the water regime should be modified. In any case, such action should be considered from the outset where the site has been drained, or where the set-aside land is surrounded by drained land. Where the field is surrounded by ditches, summer ditch levels should be penned at 20–30 cm below mean field level to encourage wading birds (Lack 1992). Detailed prescriptions similar to those used in ESAs may be suitable. Where the field is not surrounded by ditches but is underdrained, the outlet pipes can be (temporarily) blocked and mole drains ploughed in or allowed to silt up. In either case, the set-aside land may have to be isolated hydrologically to maintain high production in adjacent land where water table control is needed. However, isolation could require the digging of new ditches parallel to those existing and may be considered too expensive or undesirable if an early return to arable land is envisaged.

Aim of management
To establish a species-rich hay meadow sward without either potential weeds (both of arable and grassland) or the dominance of agriculturally productive species.

Options for follow-up management
Should the site be returned to arable production, the application of high fertilizer levels should be discouraged. If possible, headlands and ditch banks supporting the wet grassland should be retained. Such fragments would not only conserve the target habitat but potentially act as nuclei for the natural spread of wet grassland in any subsequent phase of set-aside.

Alternatively, if the land is taken out of the set-aside scheme, the quality of the grassland can be enhanced by replacing the mowing with a grazing regime, which can maintain the correct sward height for breeding waders and ducks, without the risk of harm (direct or indirect because of exposure to predators) to chicks caused by mowing. Grazing should be delayed until late May or early June. The stocking density is critical; if it is too high, there will be losses due to trampling, and the sward will be too short for many species (Lack 1992).

Financial implications (capital and recurrent costs)
Costs depend upon the management options adopted. Wild flower seed mixtures are more expensive than agricultural mixtures. The spreading of hay from existing sites is unlikely to be free of financial cost. The mowing of the site must be paid for, and more frequent mowing will be required to establish wild flower mixtures. The destruction of underdrainage has an immediate cost and, if more ambitious management of the water regime is considered, there will be cost implications in pumps and in ditch digging and management.

Potential off-site implications of different options
Set-aside involves the reduction of chemical inputs, and wetlands (including wet grasslands) remove nutrients from the drainage water. The cost of water treatment should, therefore, be reduced.

Where the water regime of the set-aside fields is altered, this may affect the drainage of adjacent land, resulting in reduced production or in the increased use of pumps to remove excess water. There may need to be consultation with the National Rivers Authority or local Internal Drainage Board.

Procedures and problems for the return to arable land
Even where wild flower mixtures are used, weeds such as couch-grasses (*Elymus* spp.) and docks (*Rumex* spp.) may become established. Other wetland species, such as rushes (*Juncus* spp.), are potential weeds of pasture, but are unlikely to pose problems in arable land. The restoration of underdrainage will frequently require an entirely new scheme, or at least new moling. If the land is adjacent to high-quality wetlands, a buffer area of at least 15 m should be left unploughed because of phosphate washing out of the ploughed soil.

Additional on-site implications of management
Management of hay meadows can be combined with grazing.

Timescales

The establishment of a rich sward characteristic of wet mesotrophic grassland may require from two to five years. Experience at Icklesham suggests that many bird species will arrive within two years.

Potentially damaging operations

The application of fertilizer and herbicide at any time, other than the spot treatment of notifiable weeds, is potentially damaging, as is excessive disturbance if the site is used by waterfowl and waders.

Appraisal

If successful, the site should have a species-rich sward within two to five years whose composition corresponds to National Vegetation Classification (Rodwell 1992) types MG2, MG4, MG5 or MG8-13. Such correspondence will not be exact, and the composition is unlikely to include the rarer species. Should the sward composition approach those of MG1, MG7a, MG7b, MG7e or MG7f (ie swards dominated by oat-grass (*Arrhenatherum elatius*) and perennial rye-grass (*Lolium perenne*) with no wetland component), the scheme can be considered to have failed. Appraisal should also include use of sites by waterfowl and wading birds.

Potential off-site impacts

Reduced nitrate runoff may be one potential impact, but increased drainage problems could arise on neighbouring land. Few of the component species of wet mesotrophic grassland pose weed problems in adjacent arable land.

Implications for access

Herb-rich hay meadows are very attractive and may lead to increased numbers of people wanting to visit the site. Paths could be used to localise disturbance.

References

Buse, A. 1992. Environmental effects of land use change as identified by habitat recording: a case study in the Llyn Peninsula, Wales. *Journal of Environmental Management,* **35**, 131–151.

Firbank, L.G., Arnold, H.R., Eversham, B.C., Mountford, J.O., Radford, G.L., Telfer, M.G., Treweek, J.R., Webb, N.R.C. & Wells, T.C.E. 1992. *The potential uses of set-aside land to benefit wildlife.* (NERC contract report to the Ministry of Agriculture, Fisheries and Food.) Abbots Ripton, Huntingdon: Institute of Terrestrial Ecology.

Fuller, R.M. 1987. The changing extent and conservation interest in lowland grasslands in England and Wales: a review of the grassland surveys 1930–84. *Biological Conservation,* **40**, 281–300.

Lack, P. 1992. *Birds on lowland farms.* London: HMSO.

Rodwell, J.S., ed. 1992. *Grasslands and montane communities.* Cambridge: Cambridge University Press.

13   HEATH AND SANDY GRASSLAND

Summary

Heath can only be restored as a long-term option on suitable soils (best assessed by whether or not they supported heath in the past), ideally close to current heathland. Restoration of lowland heath deals very much with the re-introduction of heather and sandy grassland, to provide a matrix for other species. This heathland community must eventually be maintained by grazing, cutting or burning. Upland heath is more likely to be restored on what is now grazing land, and so is not relevant to current set-aside programmes, but is an option under other habitat improvement schemes, where light grazing is permitted.

Introduction

Like most of the habitats described in this book, heathlands are anthropogenic in origin. Most developed following Bronze Age forest clearances which led to an open dwarf shrub community maintained by land uses which became traditional – rough grazing of cattle and ponies in the lowlands, sheep in the uplands, turf cutting, bracken (*Pteridium aquilinum*) cutting and fuel (gorse (*Ulex europaeus*)) gathering. These activities kept the nutrient status low while removing emergent vegetation.

There is no distinction in vegetation terms between lowland and upland heath – they form a continuum. In practice, they must be regarded separately because, of the 85–90 % of heath in the lowlands (ie below about 250 m) which has been lost, much has been converted to grasslands or arable land, and so there is scope for targeting under the set-aside regime. Heath in the uplands has been lost more to overgrazing and afforestation, and so is less appropriate to set-aside, but may well be suitable for the Habitat Scheme and other programmes. The proposals here are more pertinent to lowland than upland heath, reflecting our concern with arable set-aside.

Lowland heath can be roughly classified into dry heath, humid heath, wet peat and valley mire; they are often found together in a catchment, with a gradient from dry heath to valley mire going down the slope. Unlike wet heaths, dry heaths can be created in isolation; the other heath types may require large areas of land and the restoration of topography as well as of vegetation.

Lowland heath supports acid, sandy grassland vegetation and associated insects as well as shrubs, especially in early successional stages. It is a valuable habitat for reptiles, amphibia and many birds. The restoration of heathland should, therefore, not be restricted to attempting to create monocultures of heather (*Calluna vulgaris*), but sandy grassland should also be introduced. More complex restoration schemes involving scrub and woodland encroachment and areas of open water will benefit rare birds and dragonflies. In the uplands, however, the dwarf shrub component should typically exceed 75%; even heather monocultures would be used by moorland birds and would be highly valued for access and shooting.

Sandy, or acid, grassland is a worthwhile habitat in its own right, and is noted as an option for non-rotational set-aside. It can be created by natural regeneration in some areas, and can be introduced on appropriate soils elsewhere by sowing.

Criteria for site selection

Suitability can be judged on the basis of whether the site has been heathland in the past. If so, restoration should be considered, providing the site is large enough and especially if it adjoins existing heath.

Information necessary to identify and define suitable sites

Target habitat   In the lowlands, heath and sandy grassland; if there is space, there should also be areas of scrub and ponds. In the uplands, a more uniform stand of heather is more acceptable.

| **Location of site** | The site should ideally form a catchment which was once heathland. It should be on appropriate soils (a good indicator is whether the site has been heath in the past), and ideally close or adjacent to existing heathlands. |

A number of species, notably nightjar (*Caprimulgus europaeus*) and woodlark (*Lullula arborea*) require heath/woodland borders (both coniferous and deciduous); heaths planted next to woodlands would be especially valuable.

Small patches of heathland are particularly prone to invasion by neighbouring vegetation; set-aside may prove valuable for providing buffer areas around existing heath, into which the heath can gradually develop.

Sandy grassland restoration can be undertaken without attempting to restore heath as well; locations should again be determined by the existence of the habitat in the past and, ideally, still existing on adjacent land.

Location of site in relation to target habitat distribution

Lowland heaths and sandy grasslands are found in southern and eastern England, with small scattered fragments in the Midlands and Lancashire. Upland heaths are found in the south-west and the north.

Information necessary to assess the suitability of the site for restoration to target habitat type

Size

Sites should be at least 10 ha to be managed as a lowland heathland community (Webb &

Vermaat 1990), unless being used to extend existing heathland or to provide part of a habitat network designed to conserve particular species. Smaller habitats, and edges of larger areas, are prone to encroachment from species in surrounding biotopes; if characteristic heathland is to be maintained, the edge effects should be minimised by setting aside large blocks which are approximately square.

Soils

Soils should be of low fertility and pH, although management of soil status is possible to some extent before restoration (see below).

Recent management history

Land converted from lowland heath to farmland was most likely dry heath; wet heaths have often been modified less. However, if the system has been drained, then drainage must cease if the full range of heathland types is to be restored. Upland heath has been transformed into grazing land much more than arable land.

Management on adjacent land

Heathland is susceptible to inputs of fertilizer and herbicides. Heath restoration should not be contemplated if pollution from nearby intensive arable or livestock farming is likely, unless buffer zones and drainage channels are to be used.

Proximity to adjacent habitat

There are two aspects of proximity; the closer to existing heath, the easier it is for species to colonise, and the closer to existing heath the more likely it is that the soils are appropriate. Areas connecting patches of existing heath should be prioritised for heath restoration.

Checklist of additional features

The topography should form a catchment, if all lowland heath types are to be restored. Alternatively, shallow depressions of varying sizes may be dug before restoration.

Other designations/schemes

Lowland heaths are covered explicitly by the Countryside Stewardship Scheme, and are compatible with the aims of Environmentally Sensitive Areas and Nitrate Sensitive Areas.

Management

There are three ways of re-introducing dry heath vegetation into set-aside land.

The first is to allow natural regeneration and invasion. This is practical if the soil is of low fertility, is adjacent to existing heath, and has been under agriculture for less than five years, in which case there will be some regeneration from the seed bank.

The second is to use heather seed or heath litter. Heather seeds (usually the preferred source of vegetation) can be collected along with shoots by forage harvester during routine management of existing heath. The material should be used immediately, but can be stored overwinter, or even dried and baled for long-term storage. It should be applied at around 600–1000 g m^{-2}; material should cover around two or three times the area used for the initial collection. Heath litter is a more concentrated source of seeds, requiring only 100–200 g m^{-2}, and can be dried and stored. However, it is more difficult to collect; it must be collected by hand or by vacuum from recently burnt heath.

The third method is to use heather topsoil or turves. These will give good results, especially as they include species other than heather, but at the cost of harming existing heath. This method is very expensive, but has value if existing heath is about to be destroyed.

Grasses can be considered, either as nurse crops or to develop into sandy grassland, possibly as the grassland component of heath vegetation. The species sown should be found in nearby heathlands, because important plants, such as bristle agrostis (*Agrostis curtisii*), have restricted distributions in Britain (Rodwell 1991). Other suitable species include Highland bent (*Agrostis castellana*), fine-leaved sheep's fescue (*Festuca tenuifolia*), red fescue (*F. rubra commutata*), purple moor-grass (*Molinia caerulea*). Westerwolds rye-grass (an annual form of *Lolium multiflorum*) is unlikely to be suitable (Wells 1991). An example of a grass/forb mixture for acid grassland of fairly high initial fertility is given in Table 3. Of course, some of these species may well be introduced along with heather seeds in any case.

All seedlings must be protected from trampling and grazing. Weed invasion from the seed bank may be a problem; spot herbicide treatments should be considered.

Aims of management
To create a heather and/or grass matrix which can then develop into mature heathland of a range of types.

Site preparation techniques
If necessary, nutrient status can be reduced by sowing crops, hay cutting and turf stripping. Sulphur can be added to reduce pH in extreme cases.

Options for follow-up management
After ten years heather will need to be managed by burning or forage harvesting on a rotation, or low-level grazing, to maintain a diverse community (Gimingham 1992). Advice should be sought on which areas to manage. Some areas should be left unburnt and allowed to revert to scrub. Sandy grassland will benefit from autumn grazing, once established.

Financial implications (capital and recurrent costs)
Pywell (1991) has costed the restoration of Dorset heath. Costs arise from site preparation; harvesting, lifting, transporting and spreading materials; aftercare. The costs vary according to the method of preparation used. Fencing may be needed to keep out grazing animals.

Potential off-site implications of different options

Not applicable.

Procedures and problems encountered for return to arable land

Heath restoration is expensive and long term, and takes place on soils which are poor for arable farming. A return to arable farming could be achieved by clearance, ploughing and large inputs of fertilizer, but is unlikely to be economically viable under present economic regimes.

Additional on-site implications for management

Rabbits (*Oryctolagus cuniculus*) may need to be controlled as they can prevent the establishment of heath plants.

Timescales

Mature heathland vegetation takes 15–20 years to develop, longer if soil fertility must be reduced first. Experiments at ITE suggest that a sandy grassland/dwarf shrub vegetation, suitable as buffer areas around existing heath, can be achieved in three or four years on low-fertility soils.

Potentially damaging operations

Inputs of fertilizers, pesticides and herbicides are potentially damaging.

Appraisal

The National Vegetation Classification (Rodwell 1991) recognises 14 heathland types; if the vegetation falls within one of the nine major categories within 15–20 years, this may be taken as an indication of success. Potentially more rapid indicators may be given by considering the bird and invertebrate communities, or at an even earlier stage by assessing the level of heather cover.

Potential off-site impacts

These are likely to be small; heath communities are poor in species, and are more likely to be influenced by external factors than *vice versa*. Numbers of rabbits may, however, increase.

Implications for access

Heath communities cannot stand heavy use by people, but access for walkers should present no problems.

Table 3. A grass/forb mixture suitable for creating acid grassland (source: Wells 1991). This must be modified by region, as not all species are distributed across all former heathlands

Grasses Common name	Latin name	% by weight of grasses	kg ha^{-1}
Common bent-grass	*Agrostis capillaris*		
(or Highland bent	*A. castellana*)	10	2.4
Sweet vernal-grass	*Anthoxanthum odoratum*	5	1.2
Crested dog's-tail	*Cynosurus cristatus*	20	4.8
Wavy hair-grass	*Deschampsia flexuosa*	15	3.6
Sheep's fescue	*Festuca ovina*	30	7.2
Red fescue	*Festuca rubra pruinosa*	20	4.8
	Total	100	24.0

Forbs Common name	Latin name	% by weight of forbs	kg ha^{-1}
Yarrow	*Achillea millefolium*	4	240
Lesser knapwood	*Centaurea nigra*	5	300
Lady's bedstraw	*Galium verum*	5	300
Rough hawkbit	*Leontodon hispidus*	2	120
Ox-eye daisy	*Leucanthemum vulgare*	15	900
Birdsfoot-trefoil	*Lotus corniculatus*	7	420
Musk mallow	*Malva moschata*	10	600
Ribwort	*Plantago lanceolata*	10	600
Self-heal	*Prunella vulgaris*	10	600
Yellow-rattle	*Rhinanthus minor*	15	900
Betony	*Stachys officinalis*	2	120
Lesser yellow trefoil	*Trifolium dubium*	15	900
	Total	100	6000

References

Gimingham, C.H. 1992. *The lowland heath management handbook.* Peterborough: English Nature.

Pywell, R.F. 1991. Heathland translocation and restoration. In: *Proceedings of heathlands conference. II: History and management of southern lowland heaths,* edited by M.D.H. Auld, B.P. Pickess & N.D. Burgess, 18–26. Sandy: Royal Society for the Protection of Birds.

Rodwell, J.S. 1991. *Heaths and mires.* (British plant communities, Volume 2.) Cambridge: Cambridge University Press.

Webb, N.R. & Vermaat, A.H. 1990. Changes in vegetation diversity on remnant heathland fragments. *Biological Conservation,* **53**, 253–264.

Wells, T.C.E. 1991. Restoring and re-creating species-rich lowland dry grassland. In: *The conservation of lowland dry grassland birds in Europe,* edited by P.D. Goriup, L.A. Batten & J.A. Norton, 125–132. Peterborough: Joint Nature Conservation Committee.

14 SALT MARSH

Summary

The restoration of salt marsh on set-aside land is a long-term option best regarded as an integral part of a wider programme of coastal defence management. Opportunities for wildlife are great, especially if combined with nearby damp grassland. Management essentially involves breaching current sea defences and allowing the sea to wash over land in front of a new sea defence wall.

Introduction

Salt marshes are the product of dynamic systems of accretion and loss of sediments. However, in many parts of Britain, the rate of loss now exceeds the rate of accretion, so that our salt marshes are disappearing. Furthermore, salt marsh continues to be reclaimed into land. The result is a 'coastal squeeze', which will only be exacerbated by rising sea levels due to climate change and the sinking land levels in the south-east of England. Salt marshes are home to specialist plant and invertebrate communities, but are best known for the large numbers of waders, geese and ducks that breed and overwinter in their thousands. Salt marshes have potential financial benefits too, by contributing to sea defence systems. Rather than maintaining current defences, in some areas it will be far cheaper to allow the conversion of set-aside land behind the current sea wall into salt marsh in front of a new sea defence, where the marsh will tend to absorb wave energy (eg English Nature 1992). Salt marsh should be restored as part of a wider programme of coastal management.

Combinations of salt marsh, damp grassland and scrub areas will be particularly valuable for birds.

Criteria for site selection

Salt marsh restoration implies a long-term commitment, and so will be covered by the Habitat Scheme, although it is hoped that it can also count as part of the set-aside requirement for the farm. Selected sites will almost always be coastal, or immediately adjacent to tidal salt water (saline conditions occur only very locally inland). Restoration is most desirable along the south and east coasts of England, where sea defences and sinking land levels (added to the potential impact of sea level rise) have led to a reduction in the area of salt marsh.

Information necessary to identify and define suitable sites

Suitability could be determined using maps and coastal management plans.

Target habitat	Salt marsh.
Location of site	Immediately adjacent to sea defences or tidal salt water.
Location of site in relation to target habitat distribution	Dependence on saline water restricts locations to the coastal zone, often in sites only separated from extant salt marsh by sea defences. Salt marsh development could be attempted inland on suitable soils (eg over Triassic [Keuper] saliferous beds).

Information necessary to assess the suitability of the site for restoration to the target habitat type

Most sites will be unsuitable for set-aside to salt marsh simply because salt water is not available. Even in the coastal zone, protection against sea flooding may require that existing sea defences be maintained. The expense of returning salt marsh to arable production may mean that other set-aside options are preferred.

Size	Although most sizes of site are suitable, creation of salt marsh would be most appropriate over larger areas where the expense of sea water

control can be justified and a variety of halophytic communities (from pioneer to closed swards) might have space to develop.

Soils
Development of salt marsh will be most successful on groundwater gleys derived from marine alluvium, but may also be attempted on stagnogleys of the Salop association, provided there is saline groundwater.

Recent management history
Sites where control of salt water (either marine or estuarine) has been necessary will be most suitable and may potentially be converted to salt marsh simply by the relaxation of such control. Sites where fertilizer and herbicide inputs have been low will be most appropriate

Management on adjacent land
This aspect is not generally applicable, though control of fresh water and nutrient inputs from adjacent land on to the set-aside land may be required. Damp grassland and scrub would be valuable adjacent habitats for birds.

Proximity to existing habitat
Provided there is a supply of salt water, existing habitat need not be close to the set-aside land. However, in most cases, natural salt marsh will be nearby and, particularly if tidal water is allowed to move from existing to set-aside salt marsh, may behave as a source of plant propagules.

Checklist of additional features

If it is proposed that sea defences are breached to create new salt marsh, the implications for flood control in the area should be assessed. The coastal sediment supply must be adequate; if the salt marsh is to be sustained, there should be no net loss of sediment from the area.

Other designations/schemes
Existing salt marsh is covered by the Countryside Stewardship Scheme.

Management

The altitude of the proposed site relative to nearby salt marsh should be checked. After reclamation, the land level may sink, creating tidal mudflats rather than salt marsh. If the set-aside land lies behind sea defences and is not isolated from other areas by natural high ground, some barrier must be erected at the landward side. This may take the form of an earth bund or a dyke that could receive any salt water supplied. A branching creek system must be created to drain the new marsh. Salt water could be provided by opening the sea defences (sluice or breached wall) to allow normal tidal flow over the site or by pumping sea water directly on to the site to a regular or *ad hoc* timetable. The second option might also be used where no sea wall exists (where the set-aside land directly borders an estuary and/ or the upper levels of existing salt marsh). Salt water should be introduced as soon as possible after harvest. Following the provision of salt water, little additional management will be required, as most weed species and natural colonists of abandoned fields cannot tolerate the saline conditions. The duration of any salt water inundation will determine which communities develop. Including land with varied microtopography or creating temporary depressions and ridges will provide opportunities for restoring a diversity of salt marsh types. Plant material harvested from existing salt marshes could be scattered over the site to provide a seed source.

Aim of management
To develop a diverse halophytic vegetation.

Options for follow-up management
Light grazing may be adopted. The site could also be used as a nature reserve area.

Financial implications (capital and recurrent costs)

There may be considerable outlay in isolating the site from adjacent farmland or if substantial repairs are required to the sea defences. Although capital outlay in pumping sea water on to the site will be less, this option will incur regular costs in fuel and maintenance.

Potential off-site implications of different options

The construction of a barrier to salt water may take some additional land out of production. If no barrier is built, then there is a risk that salt water will influence adjacent farmland. New sea walls may be required in any case to compensate for sinking land level and sea level rise, and the opportunity may then arise to create salt marsh. However, such sites are likely to be permanent.

Procedures and problems encountered for return to arable land

Salt marsh would be difficult to return to arable production. If this is desired, any barrier constructed will be removed and any breach in the sea defences closed. Soil structure may have been destroyed by the addition of salt, and some remedial action (possibly involving the introduction of organic matter) may be required. The land may have to be left uncultivated for a period after set-aside to allow residual salt to be leached from the soil. Alternatively, the land might be temporarily sown with a salt-tolerant grass mixture and cut or grazed.

After reversion to arable cultivation, small areas (pools or ditches) might be retained. Salt water could be pumped periodically into these watercourses to maintain saline conditions. Future use of the land might be of a less intensive type, where residual salinity would not be such a problem to cultivation. Alternatively, the site could be used for the cultivation of salt-tolerant crops (eg beet, cabbage, kale or asparagus).

Additional on-site implications of management

Salt marsh will provide grazing and other feeding opportunities for waterfowl and waders. It may also protect housing and productive agriculture from flooding and storm damage.

Timescales

Because of the possible need for engineering works and problems with rehabilitating the land for agriculture, set-aside for salt marsh is a long-term option. The site should have a partial cover of halophytic species after two seasons, unless propagules are introduced, where more rapid results should be expected.

Appraisal

Vegetation comparable with communities of the Spartinetea and particularly the Asteretea should be the objective. Ducks, geese and waders should use the sites within three years.

Potential off-site impacts

There are likely to be changes in the flooding regime and salinity, although the nature of these impacts will depend on the options taken. Geese may overspill to graze on adjacent farmland.

Implications for access

Land flooded (even intermittently) by salt water will be less accessible for machinery, stock and people. The mechanical properties of the soil may be altered by saline conditions, making access still more difficult. If desired, raised walks could be created, along with hides and viewing points.

Reference

English Nature. 1992. *Coastal zone conservation: English Nature's rationale, objectives and practical recommendations.* Peterborough: English Nature.

ENHANCING SET-ASIDE LAND FOR WILDLIFE

15   ADDITIONAL MEASURES

All the schemes can be enhanced by additional measures.

Pond creation

Ponds, pits, dells and other water-filled holes in the ground have a
rich and varied history, and a variety of uses (Rackham 1986).
However, pools are no longer needed for steam engines, and
drinking water for livestock is now readily available from piped
water supplies. While it is difficult to assess the national loss of
pools, it has clearly been heavy. Pond creation will promote
amphibia, grass snakes (*Natrix natrix*), birds and insects (notably
dragonflies) in areas unsuited to the restoration of ditches, berms
and damp grassland. Ponds cannot be created under the rules of
set-aside, but may be appropriate on spare land near set-aside
areas, or exemptions can be sought.

The use of pools by amphibians is positively correlated with
surface area and depth for well-established pools, and with the
presence of emergent vegetation and the proximity of woodland or
similar shelter for newly established pools (Laan & Verboom
1990). New pools can benefit early-colonising insects and those
which do not withstand the presence of fish (Jeffries 1991). The
larger the pond, the more bird species are likely to be attracted
(Lack 1992).

Ponds are most effective for conservation when arranged in multi-
pond systems of varying depth and size (up to 1 ha for birds of
open water (Osborne 1989)), allowing for a range of drying out
and vegetation management regimes. The banks should be
shallow (less than 60% slope), and isolated ponds should have a
deep-water refuge within them. Larger ponds should have bays
and even islands. Rock or wood piles should be provided
immediately adjacent to the pond for cover and hibernation for
adult amphibians. Ponds in areas of extensive wetlands can be

particularly rich in species, especially if associated with damp grasslands or water margin vegetation. Ponds should not be:

* too heavily shaded (although some overhanging trees can be used by kingfishers (*Alcedo atthis*) on larger ponds (Lack 1992));
* subject to pesticide or slurry runoff;
* used as rubbish tips, which is likely if they are close to roads or houses (Jeffries 1991).

There may need to be consultation with the National Rivers Authority when creating new ponds.

Roost and nest boxes

The tendency to tidy up the countryside, by removing derelict buildings, hedgerows and dead trees, has reduced the availability of nesting and roosting sites for species of birds and mammals. Boxes can supplement available sites for a wide range of species, from blue tits (*Parus caeruleus*) to bats, dormice (*Muscardinus avellanarius*), barn owls (*Tyto alba*), swallows (*Hirundo rustica*) and ducks.

Details of nest box design are given by Du Feu (1989); this publication deals mainly with birds, but also includes a small section on mammals. Details of boxes to provide roosting sites for bats are given by Stebbings and Walsh (1985): bearing in mind disturbance or poisoning from timber-preserving chemicals in roosts may have contributed to declines in these species, roosting boxes may be important in allowing bats to benefit from the increases of insects expected under many of the proposed set-aside options.

It should be remembered that not all boxes are used immediately, and that some timber-treatment chemicals are poisonous to mammals.

Advice can be obtained from the British Trust for Ornithology, Royal Society for the Protection of Birds and Local Naturalists' Trusts on the most appropriate provision of nest boxes.

Improving the value of non-food crops for wildlife

Environmental benefits can accrue from set-aside with alternative primary objectives. One excellent example is the use of short-rotational coppice as a non-food crop. Coppice has the potential to provide benefits for birds such as game (Foster 1992), and may acquire the rich fauna and flora associated with well-established woods. As ever, much depends upon the ability of species to disperse into the new habitats, so that coppice and other woodland planted next to existing species-rich woodland has the potential to benefit many species.

References

Du Feu, C. 1989. *Nest boxes.* (BTO guide no. 20.) Tring: British Trust for Ornithology.

Foster, C. 1992. Wood fuel production from short-rotation coppice. In: *Set-aside*, edited by J. Clarke, 215–222. Farnham: British Crop Protection Council.

Jeffries, M. 1991. The ecology and forestry conservation value of forestry ponds in Scotland, United Kingdom. *Biological Conservation,* **58**, 191–211.

Laan, R. & Verboom, B. 1990. Effects of pool size and isolation on amphibian communities. *Biological Conservation,* **54**, 251–262.

Lack, P. 1992. *Birds on lowland farms.* London: HMSO.

Osborne, P. 1989. *The management of set-aside land for birds: a practical guide.* Sandy: Royal Society for the Protection of Birds.

Rackham, O. 1986. *The history of the countryside.* London: Dent.

Stebbings, B. & Walsh, S. 1985. *Bat boxes.* London: Fauna and Flora Preservation Society.

16 CONCLUSION

Environmental set-aside will not be successful if the farmers and land users are not in agreement with its objectives. These are:

- to reduce food production within the European Community while prices to EC farmers are brought down to world levels;
- to retain arable land in good agricultural condition;
- to improve the quality of the environment.

These objectives need not be mutually exclusive, and wildlife and countryside interests should be regarded as being complementary to productive farming and agricultural policy.

In this book, we have equated environmental quality with benefits to wildlife. However, other environmental benefits include public access, reductions in nitrogen inputs and even coastal defence. For example, set-aside managed for gamebirds is beneficial to many other species; set-aside managed for geese can reduce geese grazing on crops. Field margin set-aside can help wildlife, reduce the risk of pollution of watercourses, provide access for the public and for the farmer, and even help in pest management. Also, set-aside can be used to improve the public perception of farmers, as has happened to those who have created access areas under the Countryside Premium set-aside programme.

If the environmental set-aside for conservation is widely adopted, it will result in increased diversity of landscapes at field, farm, local, regional and national levels, thus reversing a trend towards increasing specialisation of agricultural land use. It should generate landscapes which are more attractive to many people than those found in more intensively farmed areas. It will not in itself re-create traditional scenery, however; broad field margins and natural regenerated areas will create a less tidy appearance than many people (including farmers) are used to.

The benefits to wildlife can be brought about best by encouraging the development of diverse, species-rich, *untidy* landscapes. This will in turn bring about complaints of dereliction and of paying farmers to do nothing. We would argue that the production of wildlife is as valid as the production of food, and, if minimal management is good for wildlife, then untidiness should be tolerated. However, if more expensive operations are needed, such as sowing wild plants, or installing new fences and hedges, then the farmer should be compensated. The issue of dereliction should be seen with respect to the new land use; a summer chemical fallow is derelict as far as wildlife is concerned, but may look tidier than a field full of broadleaved plants, with a rich insect and bird fauna.

The creation and restoration of species-rich communities are not trivial tasks. Chalk grassland communities, for example, may take centuries to achieve maturity in terms of species composition. Policies which attempt to recreate such habitats should not simultaneously encourage the destruction of those which still exist. Set-aside can:

- allow existing habitats to expand;
- be used to provide valuable buffer zones and corridors;
- provide new sites for some species, but must not be expected to replace completely those habitats which have been lost.

Inevitably, problems will arise because management recommendations turn out to be wrong, or because they are wrongly applied. They can best be addressed by ensuring that everyone understands the principles and purposes of the management, that advice is easily available, and that there is feedback from farmers and advisors into planning, advice and documentation.

There are substantial areas of doubt and ignorance concerning the programmes we have suggested. For example, the need to reduce fertility on ex-arable soils may not be as widespread as typically assumed. Also, the range of experience of habitat restoration varies greatly. For example, work on lowland heath restoration has concentrated on returning heather (*Calluna vulgaris*) to fairly dry sites, while damp heath restoration is much less well researched. There must be an experimental programme designed to address gaps in our current knowledge. There must also be continual feedback into the planning process of the fruits of research, monitoring and assessment.

Perhaps the most controversial aspect of our recommendations is sowing species for conservation benefits. The first issue is whether plants should be sown at all. The current distribution of plants has historical as well as ecological relevance which can be lost by indiscriminate sowing; however, it could be argued that it is reasonable to sow species in an attempt to begin to make up for recent losses. The second issue relates to the provenance of seed sources, as there is concern that genetic diversity will be lost where there is large-scale sowing. This concern can be overcome by using local sources, notably through natural regeneration from existing species-rich areas and by using seeds and mowings from nearby habitats where appropriate. English Nature and County Naturalists' Trusts may be able to provide advice. The third issue relates to the choice of species. In several sections, we have suggested species lists, but these are to be regarded as guidelines. Some species are expensive, and others are more typical of some areas than others. Further advice should be sought in selecting the final seed mixtures for a given field and a given budget.

Many of the habitats which could be restored using set-aside have traditionally been managed using grazing. Grazing is allowed on non-rotational set-aside land, but only in the autumn, and so we have concentrated on mowing. The long-term effects of substituting and supplementing grazing regimes by mowing regimes are not clear for many of the habitats we have described. Where allowed, grazing can increase plant diversity, avoids problems concerning the build-up of cuttings (although piles of rotting vegetation will be gratefully used for egg-laying by grass snakes (*Natrix natrix*)), and does not expose bird chicks to predators. However, a well-managed mowing regime may be preferrable for many species to grazing at high stocking rates.

Farming for wildlife is a new concept for many farmers, but one which will become increasingly important as agriculture shifts away from maximising production towards integrating production with social and environmental concerns. While we hope that this book is of some help in showing how farmers can improve their environment within set-aside programmes, there is far less experience in farming for wildlife than farming for more conventional forms of production. This book is, therefore, a first step only; the skills of the farmers and advisors remain paramount in managing set-aside land for wildlife.

Printed in the United Kingdom for HMSO
Dd. 296758 12/93 C9 531/3 12521